Only recently have we begun ...... *eriences of girls during wars. Doree.* ...... *d smart enough - to raise the heavy c* ...... *vartime experiences. Readers will be* ...... *is gritty and humane account. A Girl's War makes so clear that in any survivor's life, "post-war" can last a long long time.*

Cynthia Enloe, Author of Nimo's War,
Emma's War: Making Feminist Sense of the Iraq War

Children occupy a paradoxical place in any society: They are invisible, powerless, voiceless and vulnerable—and yet it is they, and they alone, who will carry their nations into the future. It is appalling when governments carry out poorly conceived plans on a massive scale, such as the British WWII evacuation of city children, without a thought for how the resulting emotional damage could compromise millions of children for the rest of their lives. That the effects remained largely unstudied for decades is further evidence of poor government stewardship. There is only one thing that can shake governments out of this kind of mindset, and that is what Doreen Lehr has had the courage to do with this important book: give voice to the voiceless. This is the ultimate power and triumph of wronged children: they can bear witness. Then it is the duty of governments to listen.

Mary Edwards Wertsch,
Author of *Military Brats: Legacies of Childhood Inside the Fortress*

A Girl's War recreates a vibrant, bustling war-time Linton Camp School filled with the sound of children' voices providing happy memories to replace today's ugly school ruin. Because of the book I reconnected with a long lost school family I had not seen since those days of gas-masks and rationing. It was a harsh life and we had few home comforts, but, being older, I liked the independence and responsibility I had at the school. A Girl's War provides future generations an accurate account of the history and life at the school during WWII.

Mary Szpitter (nee Manley),
former evacuee

While Doreen researched A Girl's War I was reunited with Mr. Frank Newbould, a Linton Camp teacher who significantly influenced my life. The book creates wonderful memories of the Yorkshire Moors we children learned to love. The school, the teachers, the meals, making beds with hospital corners, the cane, the sports, the bitter cold, and a childhood that, despite war time hardships, I remember fondly.

Edward Tong,
former evacuee

A GIRL'S
WAR

A CHILDHOOD LOST
IN BRITAIN'S WWII
EVACUATION

A GIRL'S WAR

A CHILDHOOD LOST
IN BRITAIN'S WWII
EVACUATION

DOREEN DREWRY LEHR

Published by Advantage, Charleston, South Carolina.
Member of Advantage Media Group.

ADVANTAGE is a registered trademark and the Advantage colophon is a trademark of Advantage Media Group, Inc.

Printed in the United States of America.

ISBN: 978-1-59932-186-8
LCCN: 2010900758

Most Advantage Media Group titles are available at special quantity discounts for bulk purchases for sales promotions, premiums, fundraising, and educational use. Special versions or book excerpts can also be created to fit specific needs.

For more information, please write: Special Markets, Advantage Media Group, P.O. Box 272, Charleston, SC 29402 or call 1.866.775.1696.

Visit us online at **advantagefamily**.com

For the children:

Alexandra and Max;

Jamie and Lizzie

To be torn up from the roots of home life, to be sent away from the family circle, in most instances for the first time in a child's life, was a painful event. This was no social experiment; it was a surgical rent only to be contemplated as a last resort…From the first day of September 1939, evacuation ceased to a problem of administrative planning. It became instead a multitude of problems in human relationships.

R.M. Titmuss,
History of the Second World War 1950

ACKNOWLEDGMENTS

◇◇

M y grateful thanks to the Linton Residential School teachers who helped me to find those lost years and encouraged me to tell the story: Winifred Lowcock, and the late Frank Newbould, Jessie Robson, and Ailsa Williams. Also, the Linton pupils who gave generously of their time, Rose Goy, Dorothy North, Edward Tong, and to Mary Manley (Szpitter) for her endless patience.

Without the gentle prodding of Denis Boyles's, director of Brouzils Seminars, I would not have completed the book. Thank you to Hattie Boyles for her excellent attention to detail. To April Boyles for her wise counsel, warm hospitality and wonderful French meals. Also, thanks to Ferdi McDermott, principal of Chavagnes International College, Chavagnes-en-Paillers, France, for providing a comfortable place to stay, a quiet place to write, and entertainment during those necessary breaks.

I am grateful to Mr. Steve Davies and Dr. Stuart Rusby, for generously sharing their time to discuss psychological data on former evacuees. James Roffey, Evacuee Reunion Association (ERA) president, for sharing his stories, and to the ERA Staff, Karen and Jean for their time and patience, as well as to John Gould for sharing with me his extensive research on National Camp Corporation Schools.

Sara Mansfield Taber's Book Writers Class, listened to early chapters and asked to hear more; Sara Mansfield Taber, Stasha Seaton, Phyllis Whitten, Susan Robb, Kay Neer, Barbara Frechette, and Michael Scadron. To The Writers Who Don't Write who listened patiently and offered gentle criticism: Natalie Bridgewater, Michael Murray, James Mustachio, Stephen Orlovitz , and Maggie Silberstein. For the encouragement and support of, Deborah Lehr, Arletta Ciofarri, Hazel Lowe, Gwen Raaberg, Karen Schneiderman, Mary Sheerin and Anne Wallage.

A sincere thank you to the Advantage Media Group: Adam D. Witty, CEO, for assembling a superior publishing and marketing team; Gregg Stebben, COO, for being an excellent host and for providing invaluable marketing advice; Alexandria Goble, Director of Administration, who ensures the efficient operation of the group; Alison Morse, Client Services Manager, who gave generously of her time to answer all my publishing questions; Kim Hall, Creative Director, who was responsible for my wonderful book cover and for the interior design; Amy M. Ropp, Graphic Designer, who listened intently to my story in order to bring her creative ideas to my cover; Seth Rubenstein, Online Marketing and Media Manager, for my outstanding web-site and his superior media insight; and Michelle Pyle, who was always available with support and encouragement throughout the publishing process. Each of these people worked to make the publishing of my book an enjoyable experience.

TABLE OF CONTENTS

FOREWORD

◇◇◇◇◇◇◇◇◇◇◇◇◇◇◇◇◇◇◇◇◇◇◇◇◇◇◇◇◇◇◇◇◇◇◇◇

B ooks about evacuation written by ex-evacuees can often be self-indulgent and inward looking. That is not the case with this one. Doreen has been able to combine the reminiscences of her early family life with those that she experienced as an evacuee at the Linton Camp School, one of 32 such establishments built before the war for recreation purposes, but with the ulterior motive of being used to house evacuees in time of conflict. Her descriptions of life before the war, the milkman , the coalman and the trolley buses etc., is one that I can relate to in my own childhood in the 50s. This is an England that was not totally destroyed by the war, but one which is now long gone.

However, having been removed from this cosy environment and becoming one of the 1.5 million children evacuated to areas considered to be safer than where they had previously lived, Doreen suffered the emotional deprivation and uncertainty experienced by many of her generation.

It is impossible for those of us born after the war and who have not been withdrawn from the family unit for a long period of time, to empathise with the emotional trauma of family separation and the long-term effects this was to have on Doreen and her peers. One thing that is easily forgotten; with the advantage of hindsight we now know that World War II finished in 1945. When the children left home they had no idea when it would end, nor when they would return home, or indeed if their family and house would still be there. Such an experience inevitably places an indelible spot into the memory of those who took part. How they reacted to it at the time, and later, depended very much on the individual and personal circumstances. Although one cannot make generalisations about evacuation or its affects, it was to some extent a social experiment which will never again be repeated.

Doreen has given an honest account of her own anxieties during this time in Chapter 3 and how the 'authorities' at the time were too intent on giving pills rather than investigating the root cause of the problem. Such angst was shared by many of her contemporaries. Her seemingly simple nervousness about packing suitcases and the inability to 'say goodbye' are ones that I have heard expressed by hundreds of ex-evacuees I have interviewed over the past years. In a time when counselling is offered after every traumatic event, it is hard to consider that many of these children were left to cope with their emotions on their own and without any semblance of support.

This is an excellent book primarily because of its honesty. Not all ex-evacuees would be prepared to describe their lives in such an open and thought provoking way. What Doreen does is put the experience of life as an evacuee into its wider and long-term context. As a result she has not kept it to the narrow confines of a simple narrated autobiography. This will certainly go onto my students' reading list.

It is worth remembering that for a majority of those living at the time the war really did finish in 1945, but for many of the evacuees, like Doreen, the war has never ended.

Dr Martin Parsons,
Director of the Research Centre for
Evacuee and War Child Studies,
University of Reading

INTRODUCTION

<><><><><><><><><><><><><><><><><><><><><><><><><>

On 1 September 1939, the first day of the Second World War, the words "Evacuate Forthwith" launched Operation Pied Piper, at the time the largest movement of people in the history of the world. In anticipation of the German bombardment of the British Isles that began in earnest in 1940, the British government evacuated over 3.5 million people from its largest cities and sent them out into the countryside.

Almost 1.5 million of these evacuees were children, age eighteen months to fifteen years, each carrying a gasmask and wearing an identity label. Later in the war, I was one of them. I was three or four years old.

The usual account of working-class British children brought from the slums of London to middle and upper class homes in the countryside is the charming stereotype. It is not accurate. The evacuated children came from all strata of British society and from several British cities. All these young people were separated from everything familiar, family, home, school and community. For some, the experience was a positive one. For others, including me, the evacuation was a traumatic experience, one that left many of us afraid, skeptical of the kindness of strangers, with a lack of trust and emotional issues that have affected our adult lives.

The British propaganda about the evacuation was on the radio, in magazines and newspapers and on hoardings covered with posters.

However, the aim was not just to rescue children from German bombs. It was to concentrate the energy of Britain to fight a war for survival. Women between the ages of fifteen and forty-five had to work for the war effort. Mothers who evacuated their children could more easily work to support the war.

My mother faced the dilemma of being with my father during his last days or staying home with her children and having no income. During wartime, there were no social programs. The government propaganda that it was a "brave and self-sacrificing gesture" or "a fine and generous thing to protect your children from the horrors of war," helped mother justify the difficult decision to send my brother and I away.

In the early 1970s, as part of my interest in military families, I attended the first military community Drug Workshop in the German countryside. During the workshop, a chaplain casually said, "For me WWII was something I read about in the newspapers."

In that moment, all the memories I had stuffed down so deeply about my time as an evacuee emerged. When it was my turn to speak I was incapable of getting out more than, "For me, WWII was not something I read about in the newspaper." Tears began to stream down my face for all those years I had held them in check. For someone who learned as a child to rein in my emotions it was a frightening experience. I knew then I would have to examine that period of my life. A few years later, I had an emotional breakdown, which the doctor directly attributed to my time as an evacuee. It has taken until 2008 for me to be able to write about those years. It is still painful.

A Girl's War is part memoir, part detective story as I set about finding witnesses to my youth, discovering the places where I had been an evacuee and filling the blanks in my memory. It is the story of a wartime experiment that was pleasant for some, but for others caused great harm. It is an examination of what happens to children separated from their parents at a young age. Most of all, it is the accumulated evidence of a childhood I missed.

I have interviewed teachers, now in their 80s and 90s, from the Linton Residential Camp School, which was specially built for evacuees such as me. I will write about the school – only a ruin of which now exists – and the teachers before they are no longer around to provide testimony. Other evacuees and I have gathered primary and secondary research that portrays the camp school when it was an active, vibrant community full of the sounds of children's voices. I recorded the sacrifices of teachers who did what they were asked with few resources in Spartan conditions and a harsh environment. I investigated the reasons parents made the heartbreaking decisions to send their children away.

Finally, I used data from the few psychologists who studied WWII evacuees during and after the war, and more recent research on adult evacuees that helps to explain why something so seemingly benign became so difficult for so many.

I have many connections in the evacuee community. I know the need for this account, and that it has a broader appeal – an appeal that will reach through time and across oceans to speak to those whose government's policies that adversely affect children. And it will have an appeal for people who recognize how a government's social experiment can result in disrupted lives years after the bombs stop falling.

Above all, *A Girl's War* validates that childhoods do matter, especially for the thousand of former evacuees, like me, who have spent their lives waiting to go home.

PART ONE

CHAPTER 1

In wartime an English childhood was a very strange thing.

This is what I do remember:

An air raid siren blasted the silence of a 1939 English winter night. Mum hurried downstairs holding me in her arms. She called to my eight-year-old brother, "Hurry, Keith, dress yourself and don't forget your gasmask." In the sparsely furnished living room, she dressed me in what she called my "siren suit." Mum grabbed my Mickey Mouse gasmask, and ran with me to the shelter next door.

Keith and I had watched our neighbor Leo Dunn digging a large hole in his back garden. He said the hole was for an air-raid shelter. He covered the hole with a curved roof and it made a shelter that Leo said would protect us from German bombs. I didn't know what bombs were.

Leo only had one leg. When Keith asked him what had happened, Leo said he lost his leg in the First World War. Keith said he knew what war was. I did not.

I was afraid of the dark. I knew that when the siren sounded mother took us down into Leo's shelter. I hated going into the darkness and the smell of dirt bothered my nose. I tried not to breathe. As mum walked down into the shelter, a single candle shone on the faces of those gathered in that dark place. I sat on Mum's knee, and Keith whispered, "Lots of worms and spiders live in the dirt." I was scared and afraid to touch anything.

Over the shelter's opening was a coal sack that flapped in the wind but did not stop the rain or snow from coming in. That night we saw a big shadow on the coal sack. The figure grew larger and larger as it came closer. It became so big that it looked like a person coming into the shelter. Leo said it was a German soldier sneaking up to grab us if we went outside. Mum was cross and said, "Leo, it's not a German, it's the neighborhood moggy." Mother shouted at the cat and it ran away.

Mother worked at night and often had to leave us alone. She told us that night that our dad was at the hospital. It was just mother, Keith and I huddled together in that cold place with our neighbors. The Dunns' two daughters, my Godmother, Vera, age seventeen, and my namesake, Doreen, age fifteen, didn't come to the shelter. Mum said they worked all night in a factory, "doing their bit for the war."

The rumble of airplanes grew louder and louder. We put our hands over our ears. We saw rather than heard the huge explosion. "Look Mum," Keith shouted, "it looks just like fireworks." For a short time, it looked like day outside. I trembled and clung to my mother.

We lived on a council estate where all the homes were the same, with small kitchens, and living rooms with fireplaces. In the downstairs bathroom, mum lit the water heater with a match. It made the most awful bang, scaring us almost as much as the sirens or German bombs.

Upstairs were three small bedrooms and a toilet at the top of the stairs. The only heat came from the one small coal fire in the living room, leaving the rest of the house cold in winter and the bedrooms with frost on the inside of the windows.

Mum washed the clothes by hand in a large steel tub with a dolly board on which she scrubbed them. She put the wet clothes through a wooden mangle, so big that it took up most of the kitchen. Sometimes mum let me help her push the handle and watch as the big rollers squeezed the water out of the clothes. Then she hung them on a line in the garden to dry.

In all of our houses mum had what she called "a glory hole," a place to put odd items, until she found a home for them. One day, mother could not find me and she searched the neighborhood, getting her friends to help. After an anxious couple of hours, she found me asleep in the glory hole, completely covered by a huge pile of dirty washing.

All of the houses on the estate had narrow front gardens with small paths leading to wooden gates. The Dunns' garden was pretty, with a small lawn and flowers. Until my father became really sick he loved to garden, but as his health failed he did not have the time or energy to mow grass or tend flowers. Keith said, "Our back garden looks like a jungle." It was a sea of long grass, much higher than my head. Keith told me, "Wild animals live in the grass and will get you if you go in there." I never walked through it.

Mother was only five feet tall, but formidable if anyone threatened her family. She had jet-black hair and lovely blue eyes. She smelled of Evening-in-Paris. Her legs were heavy, like the rest of her body, but she could walk so fast it was hard for me to keep up with her. Keith said,

"Mum says what she thinks and is good to everybody." He said he was going to buy her a fur coat when he grew up.

Mum had little time to fuss over her appearance. I would watch her getting ready in the mornings. She cut off the top of an old stocking, put it over her head and tucked all her black hair up over it. The "Victory Roll" stood up around her head like a crown. It was fun to watch Mother do her hair. I wanted to be like her when I grew up.

Mum never shouted at us and never swore but sometimes she said, "Damn! There, you made me swear!"

She never sat idle, but had a pair of needles in her hands, knitting most of my clothes and my father's and brother's jumpers, socks and gloves. She would take me with her to the Brighouse mill, with its huge, noisy cobblestone yard, where she bought inexpensive knitting wool. The factory "girls" in their green overalls with matching green scarves covering their hair, would wheel huge skips of wool across the cobblestones. On their breaks the mill girls would come into the yard to drink tea and smoke cigarettes. They made a fuss of me and even gave me rides in the wool basket. The girls would offer mum a cigarette and she would smoke and talk with them until they went back to work.

Most evenings I would watch mum dress in her nurse's uniform, a navy blue dress with white collar and cuffs, a white cap, and a blue belt with a silver buckle. On chilly days, she wore a short navy cape lined in red. Mum was a night nurse and worked each night when we were asleep. I knew that when it got dark she would not be there. Sometimes my father stayed with us, but if he was in the hospital, it was just Keith and me.

When my Dad was ill for a long time, Mum would do other jobs. One Christmas she delivered the post. I remember sitting on a small stool near the door winding wool around a needle in an attempt to knit. I have a vivid memory of her coming through the door, the cold air rushing in behind her, snow clinging to her hat, coat, and face. I was always so excited to see her.

Sometimes I went shopping with mother. She queued a lot for bread or oranges. Mother said she would join a queue, and ask what she was waiting for once she had her place. Often she didn't want whatever it was the grocer was selling but she traded the food for things she did want from the Dunns or other neighbors.

New clothes were hard to find and we only had a few clothing coupons each month. Everyone said we had to make do and mend. Mum and her friends would go to jumble sales and exchange clothing and shoes. The women came to our house and "turned" worn out sheets and collars to make garments last longer. Some of the women used the inside material from old clothes to make new ones.

When a neighbor's daughter married, someone gave her mother some parachute silk. The girl didn't like the beige color so they dyed it blue. All the women, including mother, helped to make her wedding dress. Mrs Dunn asked mum for some of her food coupons so the girl could make a wedding cake. Mum said the neighbors helped each other out with weddings and birthdays.

A friend of mother's made leather handbags and she gave me one for Christmas. It was brown with red stitching. I was very proud of it and carried it for many years.

I thought Vera Dunn was beautiful and always wanted to go to the house when she was there. If the Dunn girls were going out in the evening, they would let me watch them get ready. I loved to see them doing their hair and putting on their makeup. They said they bought the makeup at Woolworth's. They would paint their legs with make-up from a big lemonade bottle and use a pencil to make a line on the back of their legs. When I asked what they were doing, they said, "We can't buy stockings so we paint our legs and draw on the seams so it looks like we are wearing them." I thought they spent a lot of time making stockings on their legs, but was sure I would do it just like Vera when I was a big girl.

Vera was going to marry Stanley. We liked Stanley because when he came to the house he played with us. Stanley was a big teddy bear of a man, gentle when he played with me. I enjoyed being with him because we so seldom saw or had the opportunity to play with our father. He would throw the ball for me and sometimes play hide-and-seek in the Dunns' house. Stanley played cricket and soccer in the street with Keith. Stanley's father was a butcher and Mrs. Dunn said the only reason Leo wanted Vera to marry Stanley was "because he always brings us meat when he comes to see her."

My brother, Keith, who was six years older than me, took care of me while Mum worked. She said he was the man of the house when my father was not around, which was often. While Mum was away, I remember Keith chasing me and when he caught me, he would bite my little finger until it hurt and I began to cry.

When Keith took care of me, he said he would rather be "lakin" (playing) with his friends. He even missed school to look after me. On Sundays, he would walk with me, or rather, a few yards in front of me, the two miles to Wyke Methodist Church Sunday School. He would say, "Do stop dawdling and hurry up." Because I walked so slowly, we never got there until after the class had begun.

When we had used our weekly sweet ration, Keith and I would buy lemonade powder from the Leggate sisters' sweet shop, across the road from our house. One of the sisters would give us a cone of paper with an ounce of lemonade powder inside. We would dip our fingers into it until they were bright yellow and the paper was worn through. Keith did not mind watching me if we went to the sweet shop, because the sisters would give us extra sweets. I liked humbugs and pear drops and they would always give us some if I was with him.

Keith made a cart out of old pram wheels to run errands for mum. Sometimes Keith would take me and a friend to the garage, where he took the big radio battery. When they had "topped up" the battery, the men put it onto the cart for Keith and his friend to pull the cart home. If the battery fell off the cart, Keith would need help to put it back on. It took a long time to get home. When he reached our house Leo, or one of the other neighbors, would carry the battery into the house for him.

Every morning, I would hear the rattle of the bottles as the milkman walked up the path, when it was still dark. Even during the war, our milkman, sometimes a milk lady, would deliver milk to the house. Mum loved to take the cream from the top of the milk for her first cup of tea.

A coalman also brought coal but he came in the daytime. He was an old man who always had a black face and black hands. I wondered what he looked like when he was clean. If he could get clean. His horse would stop the cart on the road outside the house and he would carry sacks of coal to the coalhouse. When he tipped it out it would land with a big crash. Keith would follow the coalman's cart and collect pieces of coal he dropped during his deliveries. Keith was proud of himself when he found enough coal to keep the fire going for the evening. Both the milkman and the coalman came by horse and cart. The horses stood quietly at the curb and I ran outside to see them, wishing I had food for those old, sad looking animals. Leo would give Keith a bucket, and tell him to follow the horses to get the droppings for his garden.

My aunt Phyllis often said, "Your mother would give away her last penny, and often does." The clothes pegs Mum used to hold her washing on the line she bought from the gypsy families who carved them from odd scraps of wood. The women came around in the summer with baskets full of pegs and sprigs of lucky heather. Mother never turned these women away. She said it was unlucky. I loved to hear her talk with them, but was sorry for their children, who often didn't have shoes and wore raggedy clothes. Mum said they had "a hard life" and didn't know where they would sleep each night. She would always find something extra for the children.

Indian men in turbans also came to the house selling goods from big suitcases. Mum told us if she or dad were not home when they came, we should not answer the door and hide under the kitchen table, which we often did. When Mum was home the man would open the suitcase on the doorstep and we would watch wide-eyed at how many items were in there: buttons, ribbons, socks, gloves, scarves and other exciting goods stuffed into the well-worn interior. Mum did not buy much, because money was always scarce, but she always bought something, however small.

Mum sometimes took me on the bus to Bradford when she went to do her shopping because we had so few shops nearby. I liked to ride upstairs so I could see everything. When the bus swung around corners, I thought it would bang into the side of a house. Sitting in the front seat, you could see into the offices or houses along the way. The advertisement boards with the Bisto Kids saying "Ah, Bisto" were almost at eye level.

We passed young women wearing clogs and shawls around their shoulders pushing prams with two or more children in them. The young women often had metal curlers in their hair and cigarettes in their mouths. All the big brick buildings in Bradford were black from the smoke from "t'mills." Yorkshire folks said they looked "mucky." Mother said the mills were weaving cloth for our lads' uniforms. I wondered why the black smoke came out of the mill chimneys.

Bradford's Foster Square was a bustling place, people rushing along the streets, newspapermen shouting the latest news, and lots of buses and trams that shook and rattled on their tracks. My favorites were the trolleybuses that would glide along the road on their overhead wires. When we went to Grandmother's we rode on the trolley bus. It sounded like an animal that hissed when it started and hissed when it stopped. The best part of going to Grandmothers was the trolleybus ride.

Mum always shopped at Bradford Market. When she had finished her shopping, she would take me to Robert's Pie Shop near Kirkgate Market for lunch. In the window, in a brass container, was an enormous steaming meat and potato pie that was always bubbling. The pie's delicious smell wafted through the market, making my mouth water. The Pie Shop had old church pews for seating their backs so high I could not see over, even when I stood on the seat. For a few pennies, Robert's served large helpings of pie with mushy peas, bread and butter, and cups of tea.

In the February 23, 2004 edition of the Guardian, the reporter said that Bradford-born author W. B Priestly gave a 1939-1940 wartime radio talk the night after a bomb had dropped near Robert's Pie Shop. "Windows splintered by an air raid, but still with its daily steaming. Every puff," rumbled Priestly, "defying Hitler, Göring, and the whole gang of them." I loved the pie shop and the added bonus of being alone with Mother was a special treat.

One evening, Mum brought home a tin of American cocoa powder given out by the local church. She poured a little into our hands. I dipped my finger into it and my smile was huge when I discovered it was sweet. Our cocoa powder was not sweet. We had so few sweets or cakes that anything sugary was a treat. I will always remember the moment I tasted the sweetness of that chocolate powder.

Mum seldom complained, but often said the worst thing the government rationed was tea. Mother drank many cups of tea each day.

I have few memories of my father. When I was about three years old, I remember crossing the road with my hand in his. I like to imagine that we had been to the Leggate sisters' sweet shop, where he bought me pear drops or humbugs. I remember thinking how tall he was. He had blue eyes, fair hair, and a big dimple in his chin. My favorite time was sitting on his knee and tracing his dimple with my small fingers. I remember a gentle man with a soft voice.

Leo and Anne Dunn were kind people, who were like grandparents to me and my brother. Anne Dunn had a loud voice and seemed to fill a room when she entered it. I loved her and thought she was part of my family because we seldom saw any of our relatives. The Dunns' house smelled of furniture polish, homegrown cabbage and Brussels sprouts. The kettle was always on for a "nice cup of tea." The Dunns gave us children tea, poured into a saucer, with lots of milk and sugar, and Anne blew on it until it was cool enough to drink. With the tea, we would have a piece of homemade cake, a bun or a biscuit. Anne liked her radio shows and we would listen to *Worker's Playtime* or *Itma*. Her favorite singer was Gracie Fields. Anne explained to us that Gracie was a Yorkshire lass and she would listen to anything she sang.

In their home, the Dunns had a green art deco statue of a graceful woman holding an elegant wolfhound at arm's length. I thought the statue the most beautiful thing I had ever seen. With the statue and rugs on the floor, I believed the Dunns were wealthy. With my father so often sick, and mum working, there were no such treasures at our house. Our living room had a small gold settee and two matching chairs. We had no rugs, only lino, on our floors.

One day, Anne Dunn took me to visit the house of their neighbors, the Higginbottoms. Mr. Higginbottom worked on the railway. Unlike the Dunns, the Higginbottoms had no carpets, no rugs, not even normal furniture, just railway benches. Mrs. Dunn said, "He brings things home from the station waiting room." The house looked so bare I knew they had to be poor.

In the Dunns' back garden, they had the Anderson Shelter and Anne's clothesline that stretched over beds of assorted vegetables and fruit bushes. Sometimes Leo would let me help him dig in the garden, and pick raspberries and blackberries from the bushes. When I shelled peas with Anne, I ate more than I put into the big bowl. She didn't mind. Sometimes she also let me help her hang the washing on the clothesline. On a windy day, I loved to watch the shirts and pants fill up with air. It looked as though they were people dancing in the breeze. I didn't want to leave the Dunns and go home. I loved to spend time with them.

Leo teased us children and often threatened to take off his wooden leg and chase us with it. He used to take my brother, Keith, to his club where he would talk about the war with his army friends. My father and mother were both teetotalers and didn't believe in drinking. Father did not approve of Keith going to a club where they served alcohol. Mum said the Dunns were such good neighbors that they shouldn't complain.

One day, Mum told us that we were moving to another house on a council estate called Ravenscliffe, on the other side of Bradford. She said, "We need to move closer to the Phoenix Company where your father has a new job." I had lived all my life at the house in Wyke, which was the only home I knew. We would have to leave the Dunns. I cried when we left.

We knew no one at the new house. There were no Dunns, or even Higginbottoms. I felt abandoned. No adult to let us help them in the garden, or give us cups of tea. I felt sad.

One afternoon, soon after we had moved, Mother sent me to take scraps to a neighbor who kept a pig. Mother told us that because of the war, the country had little food for people, so pigs needed all our leftover food – we were told waste not, want not. We saved our potato peelings, tealeaves and other waste food to feed the animals. No one questioned why someone had a pig in the neighborhood, but Mother said you could get in trouble if you didn't have a license to own one.

I liked to take scraps for the animal because the owner let us watch it feed. The huge creature wallowed in the mud, snorting as he ate. I laughed at the noise he made with his big snout as he snuffled in the trough. Best of all, the "pig lady" always gave us a few sweets in return for the scraps.

That afternoon, when I came out of the small garden gate sucking happily on my sweets, I saw an ambulance outside my house, at 10 Damon Avenue. I ran toward the ambulance just in time to see my father carried from the house on a stretcher. Because so few cars were seen during wartime it had attracted a large group of what Mother called "nosy neighbors." They clustered around the ambulance, making it difficult for me to see my father. Just before the ambulance door closed, he caught a glimpse of me and waved his hand.

The hospital they took my father to was on the other side of Bradford. Mother said that, because she had to rely on buses to get there, it might as well have been the end of the earth. Mother told Keith and me that my father was very sick and she was going to take a nursing job at the same hospital so she could be near him.

My Mum had no one in the family who could or would take care of us. Her mother, my grandmother, was a tiny woman who wore high-necked black dresses with a small brooch at the neck, her silver hair pulled back into a bun. Every day, Grandmother sat in her rocking chair in the window of her house, a room that smelled of the pinks she grew in her garden. The family said she looked and acted like Queen Victoria. She was always shouting orders: "Tom, fetch me my shawl," or "Jessie, where are my glasses?"

My grandmother had four children: Annie, Vincent, Jessie Elizabeth (my mother) and, 16 years later, Howard. Grandmother said she was too busy to look after a baby. Mother said she brought Howard up.

A wartime tea at Grandmother's was Spam, salad, and bread and margarine, followed by prunes and custard. After the prunes were eaten we children would arrange the pits around the rim of the bowl and count them: "Tinker, Tailor, Soldier, Sailor, Rich Man, Poor Man, Beggar Man, Thief." Keith said what he landed on was what he would be when he grew up. "For you," he told me, "it means who you will marry."

My cousin, Brian, was often at these gatherings. More often than not, when we were ready to sit down to eat, Brian became ill with terrible stomach pains, moaning and groaning until his parents hurried him from the house. Once outside, his Mother said, "Brian was fine and asked if he could go to a friend's house for tea." Annie, his mother, worried about Brian making grandmother cross.

Grandmother herself was the only one allowed to have real sugar, rationed during the war, to sweeten her tea. I watched with big eyes as grandmother ceremoniously took the crocheted cover, weighted with colored beads at each corner, off the large glass sugar bowl. She dipped the silver sugar spoon into what looked like white sand. She made the rest of us, including Granddad, use saccharin, white pills that sizzled like Alka Seltzer and made the tea taste awful. I learned from Grandmother never to sweeten any drink.

Mother knew she could not depend on my grandmother to help with her children, whatever the circumstances.

Mother said Keith was going to a new school for evacuee children on the Yorkshire Moors. She said I was too young to go to there.

Reverend Dean, who I knew from Sunday School, had arranged for me to go to stay at a Methodist boys' boarding school. I have no memory of the parting from mother and Keith or of the journey to the school. Reverend Dean drove me there.

I do remember driving up to the big ivy-covered house with its circular drive.

Left alone in the school foyer with its large black and white tiles, I wondered what I had done to lose my mother, father, and brother in one short drive. Why, I wondered, am I the only girl in a school full of boys? What am I doing here?

CHAPTER TWO

M y parents met when my father was a patient at Beverley Tuberculosis Hospital, near Hull, Yorkshire, where mother was a nurse.

My father, Walter Drewry, was born on 24 February 1902, in Hull, a seaport where fishing had been the occupation of families for centuries. Walter was the eldest of three brothers and one sister. His mother died when the children were young. His father was a wine importer and a cooper who made the barrels used to store it. Ships from around the world docked in Hull bringing an array of goods, produce, and the inevitable sickness.

Walter trained as an engineer and as a gymnast in his spare time. At age twenty-five, he contracted tuberculosis (TB), still an incurable disease, and went for treatment to the Beverly Hospital. Britain built many such hospitals in country settings in the 1920s and 1930s because doctors believed fresh air was good for TB patients.

My mother, Jessie Elizabeth Lowe, was a nurse at the hospital. When she met my father, she had recently transferred from a local Fever Hospital after completing her nursing training. Jessie was popular among the staff and the patients, even more so when she adopted a newborn lamb whose mother had died giving birth. She fed it with a baby-bottle and the lamb followed her everywhere.

My father, a shy young man, was smitten with the black-haired, blue-eyed nurse whose affections for this needy animal he shared. When well enough to take trips outside the hospital, Walter plucked up the courage to ask Jessie out. They went out on his motorcycle with Jessie riding in the sidecar. Mum often spoke of the beautiful countryside surrounding the hospital and the picnics they shared once he was "on the mend."

The couple courted for a year before their marriage at the Shipley Methodist Mission on 22 September 1928. Walter tried to follow his profession as an engineer, but illness frequently restricted his working life.

My two brothers, Alan and Keith, were born in Wakefield, Yorkshire, before my parents moved to Wyke, a suburb of Bradford, the city where my grandparents lived.

Mother was often very sad when she saw a child who looked like my brother, Alan, who died just before I was born. Alan had appendicitis and my parents took him to Bradford Children's hospital, where he contracted peritonitis and died. He was seven years old. My mother, father and Keith were devastated.

We lived for decades with the ghost of mother's eldest child. Parents can never forget the loss of a child. On 21 August, the day he died, for the rest of her life mum would say, "Today Alan would be ten" or "Alan would have been thirty-two."

I recently discovered my grandmother had handwritten a poem by an anonymous author, at the time of Alan's death.

Alan died Aug 21-1936

> *His little tongue hath ceased to speak*
> *His hands have ceased to play*
> *From those who did him dearly love*
> *To heaven he is called away*
> *Who plucked this flower?*
> *I, said the master,*
> *The gardener held his peace.*

Maybe grandmother's indifference to her other grandchildren resulted from a fear of becoming too attached to them after the traumatic loss of her first grandchild.

The bill for Alan's funeral, dated 25 August 1936, at Westfield Independent Chapel, Wyke, was five pounds ten shillings. Five shillings was the minister's fee. Finding that amount of money must have been difficult, at a time when a workingman earned less than 20 pounds a month.

From a young age, I knew that children could die. Mother often talked about Alan and his death with her sister-in-law within my hearing. Four years later, the aunt's daughter, cousin Eunice, died at age eleven, while in the same Bradford Children's hospital, also with appendicitis. I would listen as the two women talked about the deaths of their children. I grew up terrified that I, like my brother and cousin, would get appendicitis and die.

My brother, Keith, was five years old when Alan died. Keith was inconsolable.

The brothers were like twins, except Alan had dark hair and Keith's was fair. Mother was pregnant with me and seven months after Alan's death, I was born. How sad Keith must have been to have his best friend and beloved big brother taken from him and replaced by a baby sister -- a baby, that could not play or share his adventures as Alan had done.

Grandmother's mother, my great-grandmother, Catherine Davies, was born in Wales in 1840. Mother said she was a sweet, tiny woman who always wore a white bonnet with ribbons tied under her chin. Mother remembered her fondly as "a wonderful cook." Catherine's family moved from Mold, Wales, to Hebden, a village on the southern edge of the Yorkshire Moors, when her father, John Davies, a lead mining engineer, took a job at a mine in the Grassington area. John Marshall, my great-grandfather, was a lead miner at the Appletreewick mine.

Catherine Davies and John Marshall were married at the Parish Church of St. Michael and All Angels, Linton-in-Craven, in 1867. My great-grandparents settled in Appletreewick, not far from Linton, and had four children. The eldest son, Francis Marshall, went to fight in France in World War I. Like thousands of other young soldiers, he was killed and never returned.

Catherine, like many Welsh people, was raised "chapel," and the Methodist tradition became an integral part of her life and, subsequently, the life of her daughter, my grandmother.

As a young woman, Grandmother attended a girls' finishing school where she learned millinery, embroidery, knitting and crocheting. Through two World Wars, she used her skills to clothe her family and to help the Methodist Chapel. During both conflicts, she embroidered tablecloths, pillowcases, and clothing to raffle and raise money for the war effort. She made hundreds of small, brooch-sized black felt cats, considered lucky in Britain, with jeweled eyes and tartan bows that she sold at church bazaars. She knitted balaclavas, scarves, gloves, and socks, worn by hundreds of British soldiers during both wars.

During World War II, when toys were hard to find, Grandmother made the most beautiful elephants and life sized-dogs. She kept the toys hidden from the prying eyes of her only granddaughter, who searched diligently on each visit, in an attempt to find them. When I did find one of these treasures, usually under the sofa, I would take the life-sized Scottie for a walk on its leash or play with the exquisitely-decorated elephant that she had so cleverly sewn. I never owned one of these stuffed animals, however. Grandmother gave them away as gifts to the children of her Methodist minister and her doctor.

Grandmother was a very religious woman. We knew this because she so often told us. She spent most of her days at the Methodist Mission helping raise money for the war, making tea for volunteers or rehearsing for plays and concerts in which she loved to perform. On every visit to see Grandmother, she would offer us a small box and instruct us to take a rolled piece of paper containing a religious quotation -- "Thou shalt not steal," or, "thou shalt not kill," or another of grandmother's favorite religious quotes.

Grandmother said Methodists did not drink alcohol, smoke ciga-rettes, dance, or gamble. For Grandmother the biggest sin was gambling and the worst-kept family secret was that Granddad loved to gamble. He would read the Yorkshire Post with the pink sports paper hidden inside. We knew Granddad gave money to a young man who placed his bets for him. No one told Grandmother.

Granddad was a quiet, good-natured man with very poor eyesight, who wore glasses with thick lenses and seldom spoke when Grandmother was around. As a young man, he won a gold medal for professional walking and in 1936, he and a friend toured the Continent on their bicycles and recorded their experiences. Until he was almost 90, Granddad cycled daily to his upholstery store in the city of Bradford. Uncle Vincent, his eldest son, said the reason Granddad pursued so many hobbies and worked so many years was to get away from Grandmother. Vincent said, "Grandmother ruined lives."

Uncle Vincent, my mother's eldest brother, was a small man with a wonderful sense of humor. He wrote jokes for comedians and some said he was the one who should have been on the stage. Grandmother took Vincent out of full time school at age ten, to work part time, in a woolen mill. He hauled large skips full of wool, a job, Mother said, that stunted his growth.

Uncle Vincent was married to Aunt Phyllis, a plain, blunt-spoken Yorkshire woman, much taller than her husband. They did not have any children, so Aunt Phyllis would occasionally take me out for tea. The family knew that Vincent had a girlfriend called Noreen, whom he met on wartime business in London. He took Noreen to Quaglino's, a well-known London restaurant, where, Mother said, "She would give her eyeteeth to eat." Aunt Annie and mother would talk about Noreen when I was in the room. Aunt Phyllis and Grandmother did not know about Noreen. Mother, her sister Annie, and I, did. We never told Grandmother.

Grandmother's youngest son, my uncle Howard, wanted to be a newspaper reporter and won a scholarship to a school that would have furthered his dream. Grandmother received the acceptance letter but never told Howard he had passed the scholarship. Instead, she insisted he leave school at fourteen to work for the local baker, delivering bread. Howard's wife, Aunt Hazel, said he was an adult before a friend of grandmother's told Howard that he had, indeed, passed the exam.

At the age of eighteen, Mother's elder sister, Annie, became engaged to a mill owner's son, who was the love of her life. Grandmother said she was too young to marry and insisted that Annie, a quiet, timid soul, break off her engagement. The young man remained a life-long bachelor. Annie did marry eventually but it was not a happy marriage.

When my Mother was an 18-year-old student nurse living in Hull, a city many miles from home, she contracted scarlet fever. The hospital Matron wrote to Grandmother and asked her to visit her daughter. Instead of visiting, my grandmother sent a letter suggesting that Jessie was faking her illness. When my Father died, Grandmother did not come to see my Mother even though they lived in the same city, nor did she offer support. Mother did not expect her mother to help with her children when her husband became ill, nor did she wish her to do so. Grandmother did indeed ruin lives.

Because my father was so often ill, it was usually mother, Keith and I in the shelter with the Dunns.

Practically every small house without a basement, and which was in an area vulnerable to air raids, had an Anderson shelter in the garden.

These shelters, made out of corrugate steel plating, were sunk into the ground, and the earth dug out to make the hole was thrown over the top and sides and patted down. [1]

People planted grass and flowers on the top and sides to form a camouflage cover. The government said the shelters would help to save lives when German bombs dropped. Unfortunately, many people discovered that with a direct hit, the shelters did not afford the protection they were promised.

Leo joked about the war and the bombing, a very British way of dealing with fear. In his 1985 book *Who Will Take Our Children*, Carlton Jackson quotes wartime children and their opinions on war. A boy called Gerald summed up the frustrations of many children when he said,

> *War's a damned nuisance: you can't get sweets. Everything's on coupons. Vera, thirteen, said, … 'It's a terrible thing war; such a waste of life and energy, and the country will suffer for years and years.' Her friend Doris, also thirteen, said, 'The war's nasty, driving you away from your own home, and you can't settle down.'* [2]

For most British children, war was unfair, confusing, and terrifying.

As a young child, I had no idea why people were dropping bombs, nor why we had to sit so often in that cold shelter with dirt walls and floor. The sirens, the shelter, the sound of bombs dropping, and the sky lighting up as though it was daytime, are memories that are as vivid today as if they happened yesterday.

My parents lived on a new estate of brick houses, each one identical to the next. These government council estates built around Britain in the 1930s and the 1940s provided housing for working families. These "new" homes had indoor plumbing, and were a big improvement over housing previously available for the British working-class.

The only way to individualize the houses was to beautify the gardens. Victory gardens were encouraged by the government so people could grow their own food. Hitler may have changed the map of Europe, but the British refused to give up their love of gardening. Every gardening triumph, whether flower or vegetable, was a way of thumbing their noses at the Germans. They could drop their bombs, but gardening was a confirmation for many that life could go on as usual. When the men left for the war, the women would dig, plant, and mow along with their other responsibilities. On each side of our unkempt jungle there were two beautifully-kept gardens.

During wartime, the women kept the home fires burning, taking over myriad male jobs in the munitions factories, on the farms, driving buses and ambulances and keeping hospitals running. Mother was a night nurse at the General Electric Company (GEC) munitions' factory.

Making family life harder was rationing on food, clothes, shoes, petrol, and even furniture built under the government's utility label. Adults and children had to have ration books and identity cards. Government radio programs taught women how to use powdered eggs and powdered milk, and how to make a fat-free cake. The government issued instructions on how to build air raid shelters, grow your own food, and even make blackout curtains. Mother got free orange juice and cod-liver oil the government provided for small children, to supplement their increasingly meager diets.

The government intruded on many areas of wartime life. One night, mother came home from work and the Air Raid Warden (ARP) told her, "You have light showing in your bathroom window. If it happens again, you'll be prosecuted." Mother had blackout curtains throughout the house, but not at the small bathroom window. Showing even a crack of light was an offense. The Air Raid Wardens were all volunteers who lived in the neighborhood.

In the event of a German invasion, to confuse and prevent the enemy finding their way around the country the government removed all road signs. They did not consider the British motorist, who, if they were fortunate enough to own a car and have enough petrol coupons, did not know if they were driving to Birmingham or Dagenham. Local people were hesitant to give directions in case the driver might be a "German spy." Stories abounded of people driving around in circles after being directed by skeptical Britons, sure that they had encountered a "suspicious foreigner." The British government mined the beaches, to prevent the Germans from landing on our shores and erected barbed wire barriers to prevent local people from walking on them.

Food rationing began on 8 January 1940, making even the preparation of meals a challenge.

On that day weekly allowances per person for butter became 4 oz, for sugar 12 oz and for bacon and ham 4 oz...On 11 March meat went on ration, but unlike the other rationed commodities it was rationed by price, not weight. The weekly allowance for an adult was 1s 10d (9p) and for a child below six 11d (4-1/2p). On 7 July tea was restricted to

2 oz per week and on the 22nd (July) cooking fats and margarine to 2 oz.[3]

For British people used to drinking tea non–stop throughout the day, tea rationing was a particular hardship. For special occasions, the women pooled their coupons to make a wedding or a birthday cake. When they could not get enough supplies to make a cake, many brides made do with a cardboard cake, which was stored, dusted off and used for the next wedding.

Because Britain is an island, most of the food came from abroad. The period between July 1940 and June 1941 saw the worst losses of food through sinking at sea of the whole war. The scarcity of supplies brought more food on to ration. In the spring of 1941, people's diet dropped to its lowest average of the war. The meat allowance was reduced and milk, fish and minor foods like jam and onions were scarce. Cheese was in such short supply that it was rationed at just 1 oz per week. Many grocers grumbled that they could not cut 1 oz rations, so it was cut once a month. [4]

America came to the rescue on 31 May 1941 with the Lend-Lease Bill, introducing us to Spam, lemonade powder, powdered eggs, powdered milk and sweet cocoa.[5] British women spent hours queuing for bread, oranges, and other hard to obtain commodities.

Women could sometimes buy lyle or rayon stockings, but silk stocking and nylons were impossible to find. American servicemen had access to nylon stockings, hard liquor, and cigarettes. For the British these were limited items. Our luxuries were more haphazard. Often gathered from a downed German plane, parachute silk was a luxury that never went to waste, as many a wartime bride could testify.

When we moved from Wyke, I left the only home and people I had ever known. We moved to a place with no Dunns, no backyard shelter, no Leggate's sweet shop, no Sunday school and no familiar streets or familiar faces.

My parents' new council house, 10 Damon Avenue, was the rent house where Ravenscliffe residents came once a week to pay for their homes. The house was similar to the other houses except that it had an extra room off the kitchen, where we spent most of our time. The front room was an office, not usable by the family. It had a long, high counter running the entire length of the room, with a little door that led to the back where the rent collector stood. Mother had agreed to keep the office clean, in return for a reduced rent.

The rent collector came once a week to collect money from a constant stream of people who, in winter, let in the snow, rain and cold through the continually opened door. I disliked rent days and hid myself when these people invaded our home.

When the air-raid siren went off, we couldn't go to the familiar, if scary, shelter Leo Dunn had built. We collected our gasmasks and ran to a long aboveground brick shelter. Everyone sat on a hard wooden slatted bench that went around the entire inside of the building. The shelter had a cement floor. It was cold, smelled funny and was full of people we did not know. It did not feel safe.

The government continually urged parents to get their children out of the cities and into the countryside to save them from the worst of the bombing. For those without radios the information passed through word-of-mouth in pubs, church halls and community centers through-out the land. Posters prominently posted in towns and cities "encour-aged" families to send their children away from home for their safety.

One showed a shadowy Hitler whispering to a mother who presumably had sent her children away to "bring them back."

———————————

On 1 September 1939, the words "evacuate forthwith" began the largest social displacement of people in British history: The voluntary evacuation of over three and a half million people, 1.5 were children, from British cities and towns to the presumed safety of the domestic countryside.

On that unseasonably hot autumn day, thousands of British children, with identifying luggage labels pinned to their coats and gasmasks hung around their necks, gathered to participate in what adults told them was "an adventure." Some of the younger children carried buckets and spades thinking they were going to the seaside. Most children had small suitcases or paper bags replete with food and a change of clothing, as they marched bravely in orderly crocodiles to buses, trains, or boats. If the parents thought the journey such a good idea, the children must have wondered why so many mothers were crying, and why some parents snatched their children back and took them home instead of letting them go on this special outing.[6]

Today, British parents adamantly state that they would never let their children go alone to live with strangers, and question how evacuee parents could have been so heartless. It is easy to judge societal behavior through the prism of hindsight and an era of heightened awareness.

Late in 1940, tons of German bombs began to drop daily on British cities. People leaving their homes after one of these nightly raids found their neighbors' houses demolished, and families they had known intimately, just a memory. The British people were not on the battlefield but the war made front lines of their homes. A retired RAF Air Commodore who lived in Kent during the war told me that he was going to school after lunch when the air-raid siren sounded. "I was half-way between home and school and didn't know which way to run to safety," he said.[7] Doreen Stafford spent the war years in Devon, and was walking in daylight along the Paignton seafront when:

"I heard a plane and saw it had a swastika on the side. I was terrified because the plane flew so low I could actually see the pilot's face."[8]

These were not isolated incidents.

War was not "over there" in a distant land, but played out in British neighborhoods, directly affecting people's lives. Devastation repeated night after night, month after month, year after year, seemingly with no end in sight. Parents were afraid to send children to school or on a simple errand. These were not the fears of irrational people. Daily, across the country German bombs killed ordinary people leading ordinary lives.

Information during wartime was scarce. British radio, cinema newsreels, and the seldom-used and often-unreliable telephone, were the only means of communication. The British population, less educated than today, was reliant on the government for news. More importantly, the average person at that time believed and trusted their government leaders. Given the uncertain future, most British parents would have done anything to save their most precious possessions: their children.

The British government encouraged women to send their children away for safety reasons. Women between the ages of 15 and 45 had to work, in some capacity, for the war effort. Women who evacuated their children were free to work in support of the war. Parents had to make hard choices, when the bombs began falling.

Winston Churchill approved the domestic evacuation of British children. He recognized that once the German army had invaded France, the trip to England was across a mere 22-mile stretch of water. However, the British evacuation never became compulsory. The Government did not want to thrust upon an unwilling nation the embarrassing images of reluctant children forced to leave their parents.

Lord Portal headed the British government's all-male evacuation committee, whose members had, no doubt, spent their early years in boarding schools, separated from their parents. Sending their children away to school at age eight was standard practice for the British upper class. In her book, *Women of the Raj*, Margaret MacMillan addressed this long accepted practice. She discussed the effects on the children of British officers serving in India when sent "Home" to boarding schools.

Except for those wives who took the opportunity to escape from their husbands and India, the separation was hard on everyone emotionally. For the children, being sent away was the greatest shock of their early lives. It was one from which some of them never really recovered; is it surprising that they found it difficult to trust anyone ever again? They went from a world that was rich in color and emotions to one that was cold and cramped. In India, they were spoiled and made much of; in England, they were thrust into a society where children were seen and not heard. They went to schools where India was to be driven out of their systems and Britain drummed in. Unless their Mothers stayed to supervise the process, it was hard for the children not to feel abandoned. Sometimes they reacted by hating their parents, sometimes, India; British mothers in India knew what their children might suffer if they left them at home, and were faced with an impossible choice: to abandon their husbands or their children…

There were children who saw their mothers or their fathers only once every three or four years… A girl whose mother did not recognize her when she finally came to visit her at her English boarding school felt that "something snapped in her heart." [9]

The evacuation committee of public (or, in American parlance, private) schoolboys attempted to put the norms of their childhood experience on a group of middle and lower class parents, for whom parting with their children was not standard practice. The committee gave little thought to the idea that because of the separation, parents and children would suffer. Nor did they anticipate the public rebellion to their evacuation plans.

Well before the war started, the British government had planned for the evacuation of individual children from the primary cities -- London, Birmingham, Sheffield, Coventry, Manchester, Liverpool, Hull, Bradford and Leeds -- to individual homes throughout Great Britain.

Despite Churchill's known opposition to overseas evacuation, the under-secretary of state for the Dominions, Geoffrey Shakespeare, established the Children's Overseas Reception Board (CORB). He organized the transportation by ship of some 3,000 children, between the ages of five and sixteen, to the United States and the British Colonial countries of Australia, Canada, New Zealand, Rhodesia, and South Africa.

Churchill expressed his disapproval in Parliament of the overseas evacuation of the country's children.

On 18 July, the same day that the Prime Minister opposed CORB in Parliament, the first batch of 82 evacuees was assembling in Liverpool. Some time that same day Churchill fired off a memo to Sir John Anderson, the Home Secretary:

I certainly do not propose to send a message by the senior [CORB] child to Mr McKenzie King [the Canadian Premier], or by the junior child either. If I sent a message by anyone, it would be that I entirely deprecate any stampede out of this country at the present time. [10]

In the summer of 1940, the Germans sank two ships carrying CORB evacuees, the Dutch-registered *Arandora Star* and the *Volendam*. Fortunately, there were no deaths of evacuee children in those incidents, but it made the British public question whether the safety of their children was worth the risk. The tragedy that ended the British government's official involvement in overseas evacuation occurred on 17 September 1940, when 77 British children perished on the *City of Benares*, a ship bound for Canada. From that time forward, there were no further official CORB evacuations.

After the official overseas government evacuations ended, another fourteen thousand children traveled to other countries, under what were termed "private arrangements." The vast majority of hosts in the United States were middle-class Americans willing to open their hearts and homes to provide these children with a safe haven. While the average American had altruistic intentions, the governments of Britain and America may have had ulterior motives.[11] The British government understood that the sinking of an American ship with the loss of children's lives would be a catalyst that would sway American public opinion to encourage its government to become a player in World War II.

King George V and Queen Elizabeth agreed with Churchill about overseas evacuations and kept their two daughters, Elizabeth and Margaret Rose, with them in Britain throughout the war. On 13 October 1940, the two princesses spoke on BBC Radio to the Nation's Children and ended with these words from Princess Elizabeth:

> *"Before I finish, I can truthfully say to you all that we children at home are full of cheerfulness and courage. We are trying to do all we can to help our gallant sailors, soldiers, and airmen. And we are trying, too, to bear our own share of the danger and sadness of war. We know, every one of us, that in the end, all will be well, for God will take care of us and give us victory and peace. And though peace comes, remember, it will be for us, the children of today, to make the world of tomorrow a better and happier place.*
>
> *My sister is by my side and we are both going to say good night to you. Come on Margaret...*
> *[Margaret:] Good night children*
> *[Elizabeth:] Good night and good luck to you all."* [12]

Despite strong denials at the time, the evacuation graphically illustrated the British class system. Thousands of children sent overseas, first through official channels, under the auspices of CORB, and later privately, were the children of the aristocracy and the upper-middle class. It cost twenty-five pounds to send a child abroad. This was a significant amount of money for the average British working-man, many of whom earned less than five pounds a week.

Martin Parsons reported that:

The private [overseas evacuation] schemes remained extremely elitist... or, in simple financial terms, those with money could afford to send their children away. In his diary the MP 'Chips' Channon described the scene at Euston Station on 24th June 1940 as the boat train for Liverpool was ready to depart: 'There was a queue of Rolls-Royces and liveried servants and mountains of trunks. It seemed that everyone we knew was there." [13]

Mother had a choice: stay with her children, or stay with her dying husband. Being a nurse, Mother had to know that my father was dying and naturally wanted to spend his final days with him. Mother also knew she had to work to put food on the table. She chose to work at the hospital where my father was a patient. She recognized that she had to find a place for her children. Keith would go to Linton Residential School on the Yorkshire Moors. I was too young to attend the Linton school with him.

CHAPTER THREE

◇◇◇

I met my husband, Second Lieutenant Wayne R. Lehr, while staying with a friend in Essex. Wayne's parents came on a trip to Europe at the beginning of the following year and attended our wedding, in Finchingfield, Essex, on 18 February 1961.

My husband was a second lieutenant when we married and a colonel when he retired from the Air Force in 1984. In those 23 years as the wife of a US Air Force officer, we lived in three countries, many areas of the United States, and traveled to over 22 countries. My husband also spent two year-long tours of duty in South East Asia.

In 1971, Wayne was a USAF major and we lived in Wiesbaden, Germany. At that time, the US military community was becoming increasingly aware of drug use among its young people. Even during daylight hours, a number of children were "sleeping" on what the locals called "Suicide Hill." The more informed individuals recognized that the young people were not sleeping but had taken or overdosed on drugs, a situation the military hospital frequently confirmed.

Fathers, with their military uniforms and short haircuts, had a hard time identifying with their children's long hair, bell-bottom pants, loud music and unconventional behavior. The two groups were complete opposites. More importantly, official and parental denial became an obstacle to getting help for these young people.

Drugs in Germany were easily accessible. Pills that required prescriptions in the U.S. were bought over-the-counter in German pharmacies. Young people could drive to countries like Holland, where drugs were freely available. Crossing the border back into Germany with the drugs was seldom a problem. Additionally, the young airmen flew to Turkey, Spain or Italy, and came back aboard military aircraft carrying drugs. One young airman was reputed to have had hashish used to sole his shoes -- which drug-sniffing military dogs quickly identified.

Many parents in the military community in the 1970s had no concept of the drug problem and, initially, did not take it seriously. Rather, as the senior general's wife told us, "We should ignore the 'bad' children and spend time and resources on the 'good' students." I soon discovered that speaking of the drug issue could bring military cocktail conversation to an abrupt halt.

In 1971, Dr. Jack Brown, a Wiesbaden High School teacher, recently arrived from California, started a drug program at the Wiesbaden Department of Defense (DOD) High School. Dr. Brown enlisted the help of the one social worker for the 10,000-strong military community, and others with an interest in working to raise awareness and provide help for the community's youth. I worked with the STOP program from its inception, and learned a great deal about drugs and their serious effects on the children and on the community.

In 1971, the US military did not have a program in Germany for its personnel, so the young airmen (women were also called airmen) regularly attended the high school meetings. The Wiesbaden DOD

High School worked closely with the Frankfurt DOD High School, where the drug problems were even more severe. One evening when we arrived at Frankfurt High School for a STOP meeting, we learned that a 14-year-old girl had died that day in the basement of the building from a drug overdose.

Dr. Brown organized a Drug Awareness Workshop at a YMCA building in the German countryside. I attended the weekend workshop with a community of approximately three hundred people from many European US bases that included doctors, social workers, chaplains, teachers, counselors, military police, and students. All participants had an interest in learning to recognize drugs and their use and to find treatment for addicts.

Each morning, we broke into pre-arranged groups of ten. Each group had a leader who set the agenda and began each session with a different question. One day the question was, "What do you remember about World War II?" We took it in turns to sit in the middle of the room and answer the question. One man said he lived in the US and, "I listened to reports of the war on the radio, but it really didn't impact my life – it was something that was happening a long way away." The next person to speak was a senior Air Force chaplain. He sat on the chair in a cavalier fashion with the back facing him, resting his chin on the chair back he said with a smile, "World War II was something I read about in the newspapers."

Those words hit me like a physical blow – I began to shake and did not hear the rest of his answer. I was trembling uncontrollably when it was my turn to answer the question. I sat in the chair, looked around the room and said, "World War II was not something I read about in the newspaper."

I could say nothing more. I broke down in public, something I had never done in my entire life, even as a child. I had no idea what was happening to me. From an early age, I had learned to mask my real feelings. I was mortified by the intensity of my reaction, and more so by my lack of control.

The war had been over for almost thirty years, and I was shocked on the effect it still had on my life.

The question asked that morning in the German countryside had unlocked a Pandora's Box of memories that, once opened, could not be put back. It was as though a dam had burst and I could not stop the tears flowing. Simultaneously, I had brief flashes of memories, of blurred and unformed images that popped into my mind at unexpected times. People, places and things from the past, sirens, shelters, the rumbling of airplanes, a house covered with ivy, cold baths, dry bread, and an overwhelming feeling of loneliness. It was as though I was watching snatches of a film about someone else's life. Yet I knew I had been there.

The images varied, but the most frequently occurring were the Yorkshire Moors, watery eggs, cabbage, figs, a teacher smacking me, the snow, the bitter cold, the chilblains, and planes flying low overhead, the sky lighting up like a firework display. Where were my parents? I wondered. Was this an orphanage? Was I an orphan?

I attempted to capture the images, but like a hummingbird, they hovered just long enough for me to be aware of them, and then were gone. Now I was not a child, but my mind continually filled with fleeting images of a childhood I could not fully recapture. Thoughts and images, submerged so deeply for almost thirty years, had been difficult to unearth. Once unlocked, however, they would not let me rest.

It was necessary for me to discover what happened during those missing years. Surely, that would answer some of my questions. Why did I find it difficult to trust people, to move from one home to another? Why did I avoid saying goodbye to people I cared for, or pack suitcases? If you lost your childhood, I wondered, did these things happen?

In 1973, my husband went on his second year-long tour to South East Asia. I moved with my daughter from Germany to England. We bought a house in Suffolk, near Lakenheath US Air Force Base, so our daughter, Deborah, could attend the Department of Defense School. We settled into our new home, where we would spend the year while Wayne was in Thailand. On the outside, everything seemed fine, but on the inside, I was continually trying to push down the persistent images of my childhood. I found it more and more difficult to keep pushing them away.

Later, visiting my mother in Devon, I would question her about what had happened to me as a child. She held fast to her silence on the subject. "We don't need to talk about the past."

I realized the war years had been a difficult time for her. She was incapable of reliving them. It was simply too painful.

Mother insisted that we had been in boarding schools, which we had, but never mentioned that we were evacuees. I asked, were we in orphanages? She said we were not. However, that thought continued to linger in my mind.

At the end of his tour, Wayne came back to Lakenheath and became a squadron commander, the ultimate job for any fighter pilot. Many of the older wives were not happy about his promotion, believing one of their husbands deserved the position. Those wives created an atmosphere we would today call "toxic."

Soon after he returned from SE Asia, there was a fighter aircraft accident in Germany. Wayne was assigned to lead the accident investigation team. Unfortunately, the wives, knowing that they could not get my husband removed, decided to take their anger out on me. They knew he was away and began a campaign of harassment. After Wayne left, the phone would repeatedly ring in the early hours of the morning. When I answered, there would be no one on the line. I received invitations to meetings and functions. When I arrived, there would be no one else there. What many young people said they encountered in junior school and high school, these women were acting out as adults. They had a lot of time on their hands and were both creative and vicious.

It was summer time, so when we realized how long Wayne would be away, my daughter and I drove to Germany to spend time with him. During the drive, I suffered a miscarriage and ended up in the Hahn Air Force Base Hospital. This left me weak and depressed. I returned to England and found it more and more difficult to cope with my duties as wife, mother and Squadron Commander's wife.

US military wives of the time provided what the British wryly referred to as "Battlefield Welfare," an expectation based solely on the husband's position, where the wife was integral to the military system. Whatever the situation – an aircraft accident, a pilot or a baby's death, a child's illness, or a wife's drinking problem – came under the purview of the senior wife. These expectations had been fact since the earliest days of the army. Regardless of background, the women had a job which they were expected to fulfill. Known as "two-for-one", this situation persisted within the US military into the 1990s. A husband whose wife did not play the military game would be told someone else could do her husband's job. Hence, few wives wanted to admit to their inability to live up to military expectations and were reluctant to seek help for health issues, particular mental health problems, or to report abusive husbands. The bottom line was that wives were careful not to do anything that might hurt their husbands' careers.

This was the beginning of a difficult time of anxiety, and a gradual slide into a depression. It took me a couple of years to come out of a period that disrupted my family life.

The situation with the wives became so bad that the wing commander ordered a lieutenant colonel's wife to return to the US. She and her children left and her husband completed his Lakenheath tour alone. The majors' and captains' wives, who were the instigators of the abuse were warned, through their husbands, about their behavior. One of the women explained the reason for their actions: "She always did everything well and always looked perfect. None of us could relate to her." In that woman's mind, perfection was a reason for bad behavior. In my world, perfection was a survival tool.

The miscarriage, followed by this harassment, led to a breakdown that totally took over my life and that of my family. Anyone who has been depressed, or has lived with a depressed individual, knows how devastating it is.

Everything is affected. I could find no happiness in my family or in any aspect of life. It was like being in a huge dark hole with no way out. I found it hard to fulfill even the smallest tasks.

One of the military doctors told my husband to leave me because, he said, "She is not likely to recover." (The military interpretation: "It might hurt your career.") Most military doctors in the mid 1970s knew, but cared little about, women's health. A Flight surgeon's main mission was to make sure the men could fly. There were no female fighter pilots. When my husband was in SE Asia, a doctor dismissed my ailment with the words, "You will feel better when your husband returns." We women were told through film, military protocol books, and official documents, that we should not "trouble" our husbands with even minor problems, "or you could be the cause of his accident."

When I married Wayne, an English friend explained that many of the wives took "drugs." Regardless of their complaints, doctors frequently gave anti-depressants to all military wives. Valium was the doctors' pill-of-choice for US military wives for decades.

One dour-looking military doctor was the only person to mention – and that in passing – that my childhood might have had some influence on my depression. "It was probably inevitable," he wrote. Unfortunately, he did not discuss my childhood in any detail, but rather ascribed little significance to a situation he either did not understand or did not consider sufficiently relevant.

At the time, the military brushed mental health issues under the carpet. For a military wife on an overseas base, with no optional care, the situation was dire. The doctor's main objective was to "fix" such women and slot them back into the system. With the exception of our Flight Surgeon, Wesley Jacobs (a heart surgeon recently recruited from the civilian world), the fact that the "military system" itself might be part of the problem did not seem to be a consideration.

One doctor wrote, "The patient presented with depressed affect and expressed feelings of hopelessness. Her symptoms had developed with gradually increasing severity over a period of time. She was treated in the outpatient mental health clinic but failed to show a response to Elavil and later a combination of Thorazine and Elavil." For some reason, I was unable to take pills, so the medications did not bring relief.

The report continued, "At the time of admission, she expressed the thought that she would never get better. She looked depressed, never showing a smile. Her physical examination and thought processes were normal." The notes mention "a good marriage and a supportive husband." They added, "She was functioning above average intellectually, with an IQ estimated in the 130-140 range."

I came away from the experience believing that I could not rely on the US military medical service for help. From that time forward, I worked on my own to understand what effect the evacuation, and the continued institutional, military system, had had on my life. I spent 1977-1978 attending college in London while my daughter went to a private American school on Wimbledon Common. We visited local tourist attractions, went to the London Theatre, and made trips to see my mother in Devon on a regular basis. At the end of August 1978, we flew to the US to join my husband at Langley Air Force Base, Virginia.

In October 1978, my mother became ill and I traveled from Virginia to England to be with her. Keith flew in from his home in Perth, Australia. It was the longest time I had been with my brother since we were children. On 2 November 1978, my mother died. We experienced the sadness of losing our mother, making funeral arrangements, and clearing her house. Although we knew many of the friends that attended the funeral, our greatest tie with our home country was broken. Despite the difficulties, Keith was a pleasure to be with and we enjoyed our time together.

The morning mum died, he said, "When I was young, I had to look after you while mother worked, so I was glad to go away to school." This was something I had not known and although I questioned him further, Keith was reluctant to talk about his childhood. We traveled to London by train, and Keith remarked on the beauty of the Devonshire countryside saying, "I love England, but will never come back here to live."

When I left from my gate at Heathrow Airport, Keith said, "Goodbye, our kid; I'll come and visit you next year in the US." My intention was to talk with him on that trip and find out about our respective childhoods, to get answers I thought he could provide.

The following summer we left for an assignment at Spangdahlem AFB, Germany. Keith was disappointed that he would not be able to visit us in Virginia with his daughter Rachel. On 11 November 1979, just over a year after mother died, I had a call from the Pentagon to say that Keith had suffered a fatal heart attack at his home in Perth. He was 47 years old. By the time the call came, it was too late for me to fly to Australia to attend the funeral.

Through the years, I had spent little time with my brother, but felt a huge sense of loss at his death. I will always be grateful for the three weeks we spent together when mother died. Keith was the last tie to my childhood. He knew the father I did not. I had hoped to form a closer relationship with him as an adult than we had had as children. At Keith's passing, that opportunity was gone. For several years, I gave up believing I could recreate my childhood.

In the 1980s and 1990s, I frequently visited the north of England, but had little idea where to begin looking for the threads of my childhood. I made visits to the Linton school, on the Yorkshire Moors, where I knew Keith and I had been pupils. It took me years to feel comfortable talking about those years and to come to terms with the pain of the subject matter.

Why is it important to attempt to find and reconstruct a lost childhood? My purpose is to show that childhoods are important and affect individuals, not just in their early lives but throughout their life spans. Wars shape people, particularly children. Many former evacuees, like me, dealt with the aftermath of not one World War, but through fathers and grandfathers, two wars fought only twenty years apart. The British government has yet to acknowledge that thousands, if not millions, of children's lives were deeply affected by sacrifices not of their choosing.

CHAPTER FOUR

I have only vague memories of the actual journey to the Methodist Boy's school but know Reverend Dean drove me there. Because he was a minister, he was one of the few people with a wartime petrol allowance. I remember riding in his car, because it was the first time I had been in one. I was initially excited about the ride, which mum said would be fun. I wonder how that three-year-old child[14] felt when the excitement of the ride was over.

Mother and Keith waved me off from the door of the house. The pleasure of being in a car overcame my fear of being alone with Reverend Dean, a man I did not know well, until I realized we were driving further away from home and I was not going back. The family had made hurried arrangements after my father went to the hospital, so no one had prepared me for the journey. I remember the terror I felt and how I longed to return home to Mother and Keith. The realization that I was driving away from everyone and everything familiar, to a place where I knew no one, was terrifying.

Although I remember little about Reverend Dean, I do recall how kind he always was. Reverend Ray, the man who married Wayne and I in Finchingfield in 1961, had worked in Bradford with Reverend

Dean. Reverend Ray and his wife, Kathy, spoke fondly of him and were not surprised to hear about his acts of kindness to my family. The Rays agreed that such acts were consistent with his generous character and reputation.

Reverend Dean told me I was going to stay with his friends. I asked why Keith was not coming too. He said, "Keith is going to a school on the Yorkshire Moors." When I asked why I could not go with him, he said, "You are too young to go there. The people I'm taking you to stay with are nice and it was kind of them to say you could come to live with them." He added, "I want you to be a good girl."

I was afraid to say anything more to Reverend Dean. Only another child abruptly taken away from everything and everyone familiar, to live amongst strangers, could understand the utter helplessness and desperation I felt. Having no choice about where it is going leaves a child with fear and a lack of trust in anything or anyone.

I remember approaching the old, imposing, ivy-covered building standing just off the road in acres of grounds. My heart sank as I realized that this was where I was to stay when Reverend Dean drove away. He explained that his friends, not he, lived in this big house. We drove around the grass and flowers in the centre of the driveway.

Even clearer memories are of the large door. Everything looked big to me – including the large black and white tiles in the foyer. I stood waiting on those tiles, longing to see a familiar face and wanting to be anywhere but there.

In January 1812, the first nine pupils to attend the school, the sons of Methodist ministers for whom the school was begun, must have stood in that same foyer and had similar thoughts. Like me, they must have wondered what to expect. The premise of most private schools in the 1800s and well beyond was that young boys needed a hard life with few comforts to turn them into men. Pupils in those early days complained that their meals were meager, and cold baths were a common occurrence. What I encountered in 1941 was a similar regime. The philosophy of many public schools even in the 1940s was to provide a Spartan environment. This was standard procedure for most British boarding schools until very recent times.

Further, Methodists did not believe in coddling children and would not, or could not, bend the rules for a young female child. We all had cold baths each morning. I still shiver at the thought of the cold water into which I was plunged daily by one of the female matrons.

After the daily bath, I dressed and gathered with the boys to clean our teeth at a fountain that stood in the middle of the washroom. There were many spigots around the fountain. Several boys could brush their teeth at once. I can still taste the dry tooth powder used to clean our teeth. It had a bad taste and gritty feeling that remained in my mouth throughout the day.

Most of the boys probably missed their sisters, and teased me mercilessly. At the fountain, they would stand behind me and pull faces in the mirror. Sometimes they took my toothbrush and ran away with it. Although they probably had no malicious intent, it was overwhelming to be constantly among so many older, mischievous boys – like having dozens of big brothers.

The younger boys sometimes came to my aid, attempting to recover whatever it was the older boys had taken. On some occasions, they would speak up for me, but rarely, because they knew that they would suffer repercussions if they did. On the odd occasion that they did come to my aid, it was a group of young boys who took on the senior boys, who, by tradition had power over them.

Before we could have breakfast, we had to take a daily run. I ran around the grassy area in the front of the school. The boys had a longer, more strenuous course, and they entered the dining room in noisy groups, panting with the exertion of their daily exercise, while I timidly walked into the dining room with the tall, elegant windows and long dining tables and sat on one of the long backless benches, trying to be invisible. The boys teased me if they noticed I was there. Always hungry, I welcomed the half slice of dry bread, half a chipolata sausage and mug of tea I received for breakfast – less food than the boys were given, because I was a small girl. The boys, all eight or older, had a whole sausage and a slice of bread, albeit without butter.

According to The Grovian: 175th Anniversary Supplement 1812-1987:

In the summer of 1822 the school day began at six o'clock in the morning and continued to nearly eight. It was then resumed again from nine o'clock to midday and from two o'clock until five o'clock in the afternoon. The breakfast for five mornings a week consisted of a piece of dry bread and a small tin of milk…On the remaining two mornings the pupils were given a plate of oatmeal porridge, with treacle. [15]

In the early 1940's, in a long-standing school tradition, the boys still received dry bread, but did get the addition of a sausage. I do not remember the oatmeal or the treacle.

The school built a Methodist chapel within the grounds in 1833. We made a visit to the chapel that was adjacent to the school every day. We walked there in a crocodile, the boys in their smart uniforms and I wearing whatever clothing mother had provided for me. Regardless of the weather, we walked along a small footpath that snaked through a wooded area to the school chapel. I always enjoyed the familiar Methodist hymns. While I listened to the sermon, however, I constantly wondered what had brought me to be in this school with all these boys. The minister said you had to ask for what you wanted. I wanted to go home.

Every day in that cold chapel, I would pray to go home. Every night I would repeat the prayer, "Please God, let me go home to my mum and dad and Keith." I was sure that if I prayed hard enough my mother would come and fetch me. When she did not come, I thought maybe I had not prayed hard enough. When I played outside, I carefully watched anyone who approached the school, thinking they might be coming to take me home.

Industrial pollution in the 1830s persuaded the staff to ban the Methodist boys from bathing in the River Aire. Some sixty years later, the Methodist hierarchy built a swimming bath and an asphalt-covered playground for the boys' use. After breakfast each morning, I had to play outside. I was able to bounce a ball that I found on the asphalt playground, which, during classes, I had to myself.

I would walk alone around the school and the grounds, which seemed to stretch for miles into the distance. Unused to such vast open spaces, the school grounds, although lovely, were intimidating. Running around them alone was not fun. Although I knew that home was out there somewhere, I had no idea where. What if I went out of the grounds and could not find my way back?

I discovered the swimming bath on one of my daily walks. I could not swim and could not go into the water because I did not have a bathing costume. Some of the younger boys said, "You're a girl and cannot swim with boys." I soon realized because I was a girl, there were many things boys could do that I could not.

When I became tired of trying to occupy my time outside, the teachers agreed that I should go into the classroom each morning with the younger boys. I was told, "You can come into the class but you have to be quiet." The teacher gave me a paper and a pencil and I tried not to fidget too much or bring attention to myself.

Each afternoon the teachers put me down for a nap in their staff room. The male teachers had been called up to fight in the war, so it was mainly female staff who came in for their afternoon tea. I usually awakened when I heard them talking and the teachers would share their cups of tea and biscuits with me. That was one of my favorite times of the day. The teachers made a fuss of me. I liked that.

My biggest fear was going to bed at night, because I slept alone in a large empty room or dormitory, not close to anyone (or so I believed), alone to wonder just what it was that I had done to lose my entire family. Had I not been good enough? Would I ever see any of them again? I did not ask and no one explained what was happening. They probably thought I was too young to understand. I was not too young to feel frightened and abandoned. I tried hard to be good, as Reverend Dean had told me to be.

I was afraid to get out of bed to go to the toilet because there was no light and no one around, so I did something that I knew was not good. If I needed to relieve myself, I did so in the bed, something I had never done before. Fear overcame embarrassment. Afraid of the dark, I would lie awake for hours until I was so exhausted I fell asleep. If I had soiled or wet my bed, the staff would be cross with me when they came to rouse me in the mornings. I was afraid that making them cross might mean I would have to stay longer at the school. However, the fear I felt each evening kept me in my bed regardless of the circumstances.

I spent many days daydreaming about going home to find mother and father waiting for me with a meal on the table. Somehow the meal – a steaming stew mother had cooked with bread fresh from the oven – was always a part of the dream. I wonder if the fact that I was always so hungry made me dream of food.

One day my mother's youngest brother, Howard, came to visit me at the school. He was a twenty-year-old soldier on his way to the Middle East. He, like the rest of the soldiers, did not know his exact destination. At the end of the war, Churchill said the troops who had been away from home the longest should be the first to come home. Aunt Hazel said that Howard returned from Egypt in 1945, on one of the first troop ships to return. He had been away from home for five years. Howard told her many times, "Doreen was a very tiny girl when I went to visit her at the school in Apperley Bridge." If Howard left England in 1940, I would have been three years old. In researching and putting together the pieces of my childhood, this was a significant piece of information. It meant I was at the school much longer, and was much younger, than I originally thought.

Howard caused a stir of excitement when he came to visit in his army uniform. The senior boys could relate to him because they were so close in age. He brought me the most beautiful china-faced doll with a soft, cuddly body. She had pretty, blonde hair and lovely clothes. I had never before owned a doll like it. I named her Lizzie and took her everywhere. My delight, however, was short-lived. I imagine the events went something like this:

One afternoon as I sat in the foyer with Lizzie one of the bigger boys snatched the doll and ran upstairs with her. Some of the smaller boys saw what had happened and ran after him, trying to get Lizzie. The boy was tall enough that he could hold the doll above his head so that the smaller boys could not reach her. The boy leaned over the balcony and threw the doll to his friend standing in the foyer below. The second boy attempted to catch the doll, but missed. Lizzie fell headfirst onto the tiles.

I can still hear the crack of breaking china. The sound and sight of the shattered doll mirrored how I felt.

The tiles were covered with small shards of china, blonde hair, and disconnected blue eyes. The smaller boys rushed down the stairs. It was too late for them to do anything. They gathered around the head-master, who had come to see what was causing the noise. The young boys were all talking at once, each one trying to get out his story. The headmaster chose one of them to tell him what happened. The boy said they had tried to prevent the bigger boy from taking the doll, but were unable to stop him. "He held the doll above his head and then threw it to his friend below. I just couldn't reach it," the young boy said.

The headmaster brought the two older boys over to me to apologize. Both boys said they were, "Sorry, they had not meant to break the doll.

It was just a joke," they explained. The younger boys did seem sorry, probably because the older boys tormented them in a similar way on a daily basis. The young boys were considered "poor sports" if they reported them for their bullying behavior. The older boys looked upset because such an infraction meant discipline was inevitable.

Strokes of the cane administered by the headmaster were a common punishment, used in a majority of both public and private British schools. However, the discipline administered to my tormentors was probably not as severe as in the earlier days of the school, as *The Grovian* reported. S.D. Waddy said, of caning in 1822:

> *"When I was a boy at the Grove, I was thrashed every day...it was too much – it did no good..." Earlier punishment included the victim being 'horsed" -- one of the biggest boys in the school took him on his back, holding him by his hands, his arms being placed around his neck, allowing the Governor to give the victim five or six strokes with a birch rod on his bare flesh.* [16]

Peter, the young boy who had tried to save Lizzie, said, "I am so sorry about your doll. I have a young sister and she would have been so upset if her doll had been broken." He added, "And she has lots of dolls." Despite my young age, I knew not to cry in front of the boys, even when they were being kind.

To cry brought more teasing. I had no idea why my family had suddenly deserted me and did not know what might trigger yet another such rejection. I tried to be quiet and good so no one would be displeased with me. That night, when no one could hear, I sobbed into my pillow for the loss of my doll, Lizzie – and for my family.

One day my Aunt Phyllis came to take me for an outing to Collinson's Café in Bradford, where a small quartet played for afternoon tea. They served the most delicious chocolate éclairs, even during those wartime years. I remember eating the éclair, which was probably the first one I had ever tasted – it was so delicious. Phyllis told me later she took me out because I "talked really Posh." To have lost the Bradfordian accent I had and acquired a more polished way of speaking confirmed that I must have been at the school longer than I thought.

Just before the 1942 Christmas holiday, I became ill with pneumonia. The doctor admitted me to the school infirmary. Eight boys with measles were already in the ward. The boys occasionally had visitors, but no one came to visit me. I wondered, yet again, what I had done, to be left so completely alone.

The eight boys who had measles knew one another and they played games. Initially, they did not have time to spend with a little girl who was unfortunate enough to be ill and share their ward. However, the nurses insisted they let me help them decorate the Christmas tree. We cut strips of paper and colored them, stuck them with paste into chains and strung them over the branches of the tree and across the room. I enjoyed doing that. Some boys did not seem to mind that I was a girl.

A boy named Brian worked with me making the chains and he said, "My parents live abroad and I was supposed to go to my aunt's for the Christmas hols. I do not know her very well so it is fine with me to stay here with my friends."

He asked, "Are your parents visiting for Christmas?"

I said, "I don't know if my parents will come. I don't know where they are." Brian assured me they would come on Christmas Day.

I contracted measles from the boys and that, combined with having pneumonia, meant that I was very ill. I was unable to take part in any games or further decorating of the ward. The boys would come to talk and ask if they could get anything for me.

When the school broke up for the Christmas holidays, the eight boys and I remained behind in the school's infirmary. The nurses tried to make things cheerful. Some of the boys' parents came to visit, but no one came to see me. What could have happened to them?

I just worried, rather than ask why my parents did not come. I never took my eyes off the door. Day after day, I watched and waited, willing a familiar face to walk through it.

On Christmas Day, Reverend Dean came though the door dressed as Santa Claus, with a big sack on his back. I was pleased to see him. I asked, "Where are my mother and father?" Reverend Dean said, "Your mother is very busy and the buses don't run on Christmas Day, so she couldn't come. She and Keith gave something to Santa to bring for you." He sat with me while I opened the Christmas stocking containing fruit and some small toys. When he had given all the boys their stockings, he left. I felt as though I would never see any of my family ever again.

What I did not know was that my father had died on 4 December 1942, probably around the time I became ill. Mother, relying on public transport and busy with funeral arrangements, was unable to visit. No family member or teacher told me about my father's death at that time or later.

Mother did tell my brother's headmaster, so Keith went home to attend the funeral. He knew his father had died. I would probably have understood if someone had tried to explain why mother could not visit me.

While it may seem strange today, it was quite common for parents of the wartime years to "protect their children" by keeping death and other unpleasant happenings from them. Mother was a product of her time and did what she believed to be in my best interest. Children did not need to hear the truth about death, or so she believed. As we know today, telling the truth to children is kinder than leaving them to imagine what may have happened. Along with many other wartime children, no adult ever told me that my father had died.

Such actions led to children, like me, who had no definition of death, imagining that it was possible for the missing parent to return.

Anna Freud and Dorothy Burlingham worked with evacuee children and in their findings stated:

For a child under three years of age it is extremely difficult to maintain a normal emotional relationship with an absent love object. ... The love of the infant for his mother is bound up with the fulfillment of these needs. If the mother is absent, the child forms, after a short period of longing, a new relationship to a substitute mother. The relation to the real mother has become unsatisfactory, and is driven from consciousness... The most serious objection against wartime evacuation of young children without their mothers is, therefore, that it produces artificial orphans. It is common knowledge that after the death of the father or mother small children behave as if their parents had just gone away. [17]

During the war years, it was almost impossible not to hear about people dying through conversation, radio, newspapers, or film newsreels. Children were not immune from such reports. If someone had told me that my father had died and mother was busy with the funeral, I may not have fully understood, but at least it would have given me a reason why mother did not visit.

Reverend Dean had buried my brother and, when informed that my father was dying, he naturally stepped in to try to help. He understood mother's need to be with my father, and kindly found me a place to live. The headmaster of the school was doing Reverend Dean a favor by taking me in during a difficult time in mother's life.

British public schools were institutions that had run in the same way for generations. During WWII, these schools had to undergo a forced change by employing female teachers to replace the male teachers who went to war. Flexibility was never a strong suit of British institutions. Change was something they kept to a minimum. The rules and regulations of schools had been in effect for generations and most saw little reason to alter them.

I feel sure the schoolteachers and staff made all the accommodations they could for a young child. They fed me, provided a place to sleep and entertained me during the day. Under such circumstances, what else could they do? With no family members to take care of me, all the parties did what they believed to be right.

The school was an excellent choice for the young boys who were eight or older, and no doubt provided a first-class education. Although the discipline was strict, it was equally so in most British schools of the time. Food rationing and shortages were a fact of life and all British families had to make do with less than they had had previously.

After I had recovered and the Christmas holidays were over, Mother did come to see me, and promised that she would move me to another school. She was appalled to learn that they had given me cold baths each morning and I had to run around the driveway in all weathers before my meager breakfast. She blamed what she called the Dickensian traditions of the school for my illness.

Mother took me with her to Linton School and appealed to Mr. Sternwhite, the headmaster, to take me as a pupil. Mr. Sternwhite explained that the school did not take children under the age of seven. Mother must have had persuasive powers, because by the time we left Mr. Sternwhite had agreed for me, age five, to join my brother at Linton School in the winter of 1943.

In a 1998 interview with the Woodhouse Grove School historian, who said he had no idea that a young child had been at the school during the war. I gave descriptions of the school and mentioned being in the infirmary over Christmas. He confirmed that the school did have its own infirmary in the early 1940s. He said, "What fun it must have been as a young child to have the run of these beautiful grounds."

CHAPTER FIVE

In 1996, my husband and I spent Christmas at the Devonshire Arms, Bolton Abbey, adjacent to the Duke of Devonshire's Hunting Lodge. My great-great grandmother, Jane Marshall, had worked as a maid for the Devonshire family there in the 1800s. It was the Duke's hunting lodge where, each autumn in the hunting season, he entertained the British gentry, including royal princes.

On the morning of Boxing Day, 26th December, a light dusting of snow covered the ground, adding to the beauty of the Moors as we drove from Bolton Abbey to Linton.

Yorkshire is a contradiction, the wild, breathtaking scenery of the Moors only a few miles from Bradford, my birthplace and heart of Britain's woolen industry and home to what William Blake called "those dark satanic mills."

A short distance from Brontë country, my great-great grandmother would have felt at home walking these beloved moors, so little have they changed since she worked at Bolton Abbey. Each turn in the road brought scenes of handmade gray-stone walls running across the landscape as far as the eye could see. Gray farmhouses tucked into dips in the rolling dales, and sheep huddled together to stay warm on that chilly morning.

The River Wharfe flows gently through the pastoral countryside. Strid Woods belongs to the Bolton Abbey estate and it is there that the gentle Wharfe becomes violent. The Strid is a narrow gorge where the river flows through a constricted opening, causing it to surge with enormous pressure into dangerous whirlpools on the river floor, some 30 feet below. To the visitor the narrow Strid chasm, just five feet across, appears deceptively easy to jump. Many brave souls have tried, only to lose their footing on the far sloping rock, and hurtle to their deaths in the roiling waters below.

Because of the Wharfe's violent reputation, we children learned, as a warning, an anonymous old couplet comparing it to the River Aire:

> *Wharfe is clear, and the Aire lithe,*
> *Where the Aire drowns one, Wharfe drowns five.*

Like the Strid the Yorkshire Moors' weather could be sunny and calm and in the blink of an eye change to wild, lashing rains or numbing cold. For centuries, the Moors and the people of the area have been an inspiration to writers like the Bronte sisters, who lived in Haworth, just a few miles from Linton. Their narratives give a clear picture of the granite-topped hillsides overlooking pastoral green valleys divided by slow and fast-flowing rivers. The inhabitants, as Emily described them in *Wuthering Heights*, were ruggedly determined, stoic, and thrifty with speech. The writer J.B. Priestley loved the moors, saying, "...every rock and clump of heather spoke to me in my own language." He expressed his belief that, "the moors, to the West Riding folk, are something more than a picnic place, a pretty bit of local countryside. They are the grand escape!" Thousands of weary mill workers referred to the

Yorkshire Moors with a fondness usually reserved for a well-loved family member.

On that cold December morning, we were enjoying the ever-changing views of the moors when suddenly we came over a hill and saw a sight that made me gasp. Linton Residential (Camp) School had burned, and the result was an eyesore. An ugly burned chimney stood amid the charred ruins of what was the dining hall. It looked like an evil symbol. For years, the staff had taken pride in keeping the school spick and span.

We stopped the car at the gate of the school, and climbed over the locked five-bar gate. Glass crunched underfoot as we walked from one wrecked building to another. The doors and windows hung from their hinges where fire, vandals and harsh weather had taken their sad toll. The stage in the assembly hall remained and I imagined children jumping from it, their laughter echoing through the buildings. An old mattress lay on the floor of one room, iron bedsteads in another, and pictures, painted by children now grown, were strewn around the rooms. We walked through what had been a well-kept, orderly school bustling with life, now an ugly blot on the landscape. With the loss of my family and separation from home, the school did not hold pleasant memories for me, but I was disturbed to see it in this desolate condition.

When I asked some local people what had happened, they said, "A group of travelers used the school buildings as a 'squat' in the 1980s, and one night they set it on fire." The people were unhappy that the Bradford council, who owned the property, had not made a decision on the future of the land. "The ugliness is a blight on the beauty of our landscape," they said.

Over the years, I questioned people about the "Linton Camp School," and even those familiar with the area did not know the story of its origins. They mainly believed what some authors have written: That the school was built to house evacuated families, who, one unenlightened person wrote, "came from the Brighton area." [18]

My research indicated that in 1939, the government had planned to build six "camps" around Britain in areas close to the sea or in pleasant surroundings. The camps' use was to provide a break for workers who had recently received paid holidays. In the event of war, the schools would house evacuee children. Linton Camp School was one of six identical schools, built on selected sites around the country. Because of the lack of knowledge about the history of the school, I knew I had to write about it before it was completely demolished.

It became the purpose of this book to discover my childhood at the school when it was a thriving community, a time when enemy planes flew overhead, children were evacuated from British cities, food was scarce and people used ration books and identity cards. My mother and brother had both died in the late 1970s, so I knew I would need to rely on others to fill in the blanks about a time that had had such a significant effect on my life. I needed to record life at the school before those associated with it were no longer around.

I made many trips over the years to the Linton-in-Craven area of the Yorkshire Moors. I asked questions, searched church records, visited the Bradford Education Department and interviewed people. Few people knew about the early years of the Linton School. So far, I have been unable to locate the school's photograph album and logbook, an Education Department requirement that provided a daily account of life at the school.

What I did discover during the process was that my ancestors, the Marshalls, had lived in the Linton-in-Craven area for generations. My great-grandparents, Catherine Davies and John Marshall, were married in 1876 at the Linton Church, a few minutes walk from the school.

Catherine lived in Hebden, and would have had to walk over the swing bridge that spanned the Wharfe River to the church where she was married. I remembered the first time I walked on that same bridge, a small child clinging to the rope sides, becoming frightened as the bridge began to swing from side to side.

Had Catherine and her fiancé, John, crossed the stepping-stones over the river, as we did when we took a short cut from the church to the Linton School? My search for my lost years had the added dimension of being a child with family ties to the area.

In the 1840 census, my great-great-grandmother Jane Marshall, then age 22, her father John, age 41, and her brother, Robert, age 20, were living in Appletreewick, not far from Linton. Included in the family was John Marshall, Jane's son, age three months. One afternoon, I searched the dusty books of births and deaths at the Burnsall Church and found Jane's son, John Marshall's, birth certificate. The child had his mother's surname and had no father listed. When I questioned the Linton Church vicar, a stocky fellow, who said he had been a Royal Air Force chaplain, he smiled and said, "If she worked at Bolton Abbey, there is a strong possibility that the father was one of the gentry who stayed at the Lodge." He added, "The maids were vulnerable to this type of abuse and had little defense. The men used the women against their will, and for them there were no repercussions. It was the women who suffered when they lost their jobs and had to depend on their communities for support."

The Vicar told me, "Normally, the young woman was forced to reveal the name of the father by the local constable, because the village did not want to pay for the child. The main reason women did not reveal the father's name was when a person of means was involved."

Young John Marshall lived with relatives in Skyreholme, Appletreewick, until his marriage. In later censuses, the family first claimed young John as nephew, and later as son of the family. However, despite several years and extensive repeated searches of marriages and deaths after the 1840 census, I have been unable to find any trace of Jane Marshall. I hoped to have more success with my search for my lost childhood.

In June 1997, I asked the Yorkshire Post newspaper to print an appeal for anyone evacuated to the Linton Camp School from 1940-45 to contact me. To my surprise, I received responses from three Linton Camp School staff members: Mr. Frank Newbould, Mrs. Winifred Lowcock, and Miss Ailsa Williams, all over 80 years old. I discovered that although they lived in close proximity, these former head teachers had not met for more than 50 years – not since ration books were a requirement, people spent nights in air-raid shelters, and they themselves were all in their 20s. They each expressed a wish to hold a reunion on my next visit.

On 7 September 1998, the four of us met at Betty's tearooms in Ilkley. Betty's Café tearooms are a Yorkshire legend. To visit one of six Betty's Cafés, you have to go to Yorkshire. There are none in any other county. Swiss confectioner, Frederick Belmont, began the business in 1919, when he took the wrong train from London and ended up in Harrogate, Yorkshire. No one knows, even today, the identity of Betty. The Betty's Café waitresses dress in black, Victorian-style ankle-length dresses, with white caps and aprons. They bustle about serving pots of tea, meals, and, the reason that most make the trip to Betty's, the dessert trolley, full of the most tempting array of delicious treats. My cousin Mary said, "If there isn't a Betty's in Heaven, I'm not going."

This quintessentially English setting seemed appropriate to talk about those past years. While enjoying their cups of tea and cakes the three octogenarians reminisced fondly about their World War II experiences and their evacuee charges at Linton Camp School. Their Yorkshire accents took me back to a time with my relatives, who all spoke as they did.

Soon after we sat down, Mr. Newbould leaned over to me and whispered, "I wouldn't have recognized Winifred, she was so good looking. She has aged, hasn't she?" I smiled because he did sound surprised. It had been over fifty-four years since he had seen Winifred, when she had been a young twenty-year-old. By 1998, all three of them had changed a great deal. Frank voiced those differences, looking back to a time when he was in his late 20s, enthusiastic and athletic with his future ahead of him. Winifred's aging forced him to acknowledge how the years had passed, when he saw she was no longer the attractive young woman of his memory.

I remembered Frank Newbould as a young man, pleasant looking, with an out-going personality. He was my brother's housemaster, and he always had a kind word for Keith's small sister. When I telephoned him in June 1997, and told him my name, he was a spritely 84 years old with an impressive memory. His immediate answer was, "You're Keith's sister," and his best friend, he said, was Philip Tasker.

He remembered that mother and I had visited him at his home in Otley. "Your mother was wearing a black armband because your father had just died, and you were in a white dress," he told me. I asked if his house was white and flat-roofed. He assured me that the house, built in the 1930s, was a vast contrast from the usual Yorkshire slate–gray stone houses. For years, I thought, Mr. Newbould's white house might have been a figment of my imagination. I was pleased to know that it was not.

Mr. Newbould explained that he was an original staff member recruited from the Bradford area to teach at Linton Camp School when it opened on 10 July 1940. The Bradford education department gave him only three days to prepare himself to begin work at the school. As well as teaching the children a complete educational curriculum, he also coached the boys' football and cricket teams. "Additionally," he added with a wry smile, "we had to cut hair and nails, anything the children needed. We were like parents."

Mr. Newbould explained that The Linton School was one of six built around Britain in 1940 by the National Camp Corporation, headed by Lord Portal. Each school, built of Canadian cedar-wood, had cost 20 thousand pounds. Their purpose was to house approximately 240 evacuee children in the event of war.

With his incredible memory, Mr. Newbould described in detail how the camp schools were built like army camps, each with six dormitories (with no running water), an "ablutions block" (that did have hot water, showers and two baths), a dining hall, clinic, an assembly hall, classrooms, and a tuckshop. There were also two bungalows, one for the headmaster and one for the camp manager who maintained the school.

The dormitories, divided into two sections, each housed 50 children and a staff member. At first, they decided to put the boys into one section and the girls in the other. Mr. Newbould said the boys had put holes in the dividing wall so they could spy on the girls. "We quickly realized our mistake," he chuckled. Initially, there were 240 children from 40 different schools, including local orphanages. He remarked that, "most of us had little teaching experience and in the beginning we had no textbooks, no paper or pencils, only an old radiogram, some rounder's equipment and a couple of footballs."

"It was hard work to take care of children, and keep them busy, from 7:30a.m. until 9:30pm., for two months without a break. We even had to sew on buttons and mend knicker elastic," he said. Because it was summertime, the staff decided to dispense with classes until September when they hoped to have more teaching supplies. I was fascinated and impressed by the accuracy of his information. He was an amazing man who, after almost sixty years, was able to recall such minute details. At Betty's that day, I learned he also had a fondness for chocolate pastries.

Mrs. Winifred Lowcock, a delightful 84-year-old was still driving. As young Winifred Hindle, she had won a Saltie (A Sir Titus Salt Scholarship) and received her degree from Birmingham University. She was teaching French and History at a Birmingham Grammar School when the war started. Winifred wrote to the Bradford district education department and requested a move closer to her family. They offered her a position at the Linton school.

Initially, Winifred explained, she thought it was a step down. Later, she admitted to being in awe of the other staff, who taught all subjects. She accepted the job. The other teachers had all taught together in the Bradford area and they knew one another. Winifred said that she felt "the odd one out." However, because of the isolation of the school, she said they were soon like a family. "We had a staff room that we made comfortable, and, despite the harsh weather and conditions, I look back on the time with great fondness," she told me.

Winifred married the son of the Linton Mill owner while teaching at Linton and had to leave when her first child was due. (Women were required to stop work when they had a child.) Winifred remembered how sad she was when she left Linton. Because her husband was in the British Army fighting overseas for most of the war her daughter was three –years old before her husband first saw her.

In 1998, Miss Ailsa Williams was a sprightly 85-year-old. She had not been a teacher, but had gone to the Linton school in 1942, two years after it opened, to coordinate work not done by the teachers. Her work included the supervision of the seamstresses, clothing replacements, laundry arrangements and general welfare work. She also relieved the nurse, sometimes taught classes, and filled in for Mr. Sternwhite's secretary, Dorothy Keddle. The teachers welcomed her, because she relieved them from having to sew on buttons, cut the children's nails and hair and myriad other trivial jobs that they were thrilled to relinquish.

Ailsa took the children on trips, took care of the American Foundation, a charity that sent used children's clothing, shoes and books. Ailsa said, "Linton changed my life. I realized that I would probably not marry and I needed a career." At the end of the war, Mr. Sternwhite recommended Ailsa for a teacher-training course when there was a shortage of teachers.

In September 2008, at the age of 94, she described the most wonderful image to me. Lord Londonderry had allowed the education department to use his home, Anwick Castle, for the teacher-training course. The classes were held in the ballroom, which was lined with mirrors. Lord Londonderry, she explained, "would suddenly appear through the mirrors." I loved that image. Lord Londonderry also gave a ball for these young people, some of whom had just returned from fighting WWII in Germany, and others like Ailsa, who had lived through the sacrifice of rationing and shortages. Ailsa said they all were so excited, but their concern, with continued clothing rationing, was what to wear. "We managed to make ourselves presentable," she said. Lord Londonderry evidently gave the young teachers a wonderful time. Ailsa remarked that it was, "an evening I will always remember."

Ailsa Williams taught in the Bradford school district for many years and, later, became headmistress of Marshalfield Infant School in Bradford. At 87 years old, she was great fun and busy with her activities in Ilkley, where she lived.

All three teachers spoke highly of Mr. Sternwhite, the headmaster. Winifred said he was "superb." She explained that he had been the headmaster of Bradford's Cathedral School, a private boy's school, before volunteering to head the Linton School. Mr. Newbould said Mr. Sternwhite was quite the disciplinarian, but he added, "We had some difficult children and it was the only way he could control them."

Winifred remembered how the headmaster insisted on treating the children with respect. "One day I was walking through a group of boys sitting on the floor and I nudged one of the out of the way with my foot," she explained. Mr. Sternwhite was annoyed and told her not to do that again, saying, "We must never be disrespectful to the children."

Ailsa Williams said it was because of Mr. Sternwhite that she had a career as a teacher, and believed that he had changed her life for the better. She added, "Although the children thought he was sometimes too hard on them, he was always fair. I think most of them admired him."

One of the first questions I asked was if I was correct in thinking that we (the evacuees) were not welcomed to the area by the local people. Both Frank and Winifred were quick to assure me that this was indeed a fact.

"They hadn't wanted us there in the first place and were determined to find fault if they could. If a few stones were missing from a wall it couldn't have been the sheep, oh no, it was those Camp kids. Anything they could blame us for, they did," Winifred said.

Winifred spoke of the closeness of the teachers, because of their isolated location, emphasized by the fact that the local people hated them. Mr. Newbould said, "They didn't like us to go to the pub and for many weeks they ignored us. Eventually, we won some of them over, but it took a while."

Winifred remembered how the vicar at the Linton Church did not welcome children from the school. She said, "He never mentioned the children nor adjusted his services for them and when we left he shook hands only with the local gentry, Mrs. Halliwell Sutcliffe and Mrs. Alderton from the manor, and ignored us." When she married the son of the owner of the Linton Mill, Winifred swore she would not enter the Linton Church until the vicar left. She proudly told me, "I did not."

Why did these talented young people volunteer to teach at a school in this scenic but bleak location? Winters often meant excessive snow and little entertainment, time off, or pay; their only transportation, a bicycle. The teachers earned 300 pounds a year plus their board and lodgings. Miss William's salary, as a welfare officer, began at 50 pounds, later raised to 80 pounds per annum.

The Yorkshire Post sent a photographer to cover our 1998 reunion at Betty's Café. He wrote that the last time these three educators had met, German aircraft were bombing British cities and the evacuation of children was part of the fabric of life. The Yorkshire Post put a photograph of the occasion in the newspaper. Responses poured in from some of the pupils of the time who did not know these former teachers were still around. Frank had calls from former students, as did Winifred, and Ailsa was contacted by a cousin with whom she had lost touch. They were all thrilled with the result of our Betty's reunion.

Shortly after the reunion, one of the students told me that Mrs. Jessie Robson, the wife of the headmaster who had taken over when Mr. Sternwhite retired, lived in Threshfield, close to Linton. Jessie had also been a teacher at the school during those wartime years. I made contact with Jessie and she added significantly to the information about life at the school.

Jessie had gone to Darlington Teacher's Training College. She began her career teaching at Thornbury Girl's School, Bradford and went to Linton in 1943. "I was a floater, a teacher who relieved the others when they went on holiday," she said. Jessie was the youngest teacher. The school had a number of difficult children and one girl in particular with whom the other teachers had difficulties. She was a young woman called Chrissie. The girl took a liking to Jessie, a teacher not too much older than her. "She would just be there when I was walking from building to building, and she would come to walk with me," Jessie explained. "I knew her mother was blind and I felt sorry for her. She was a smart girl who seemed to need a friend and I never had a problem with her."

The older teachers evidently objected to Jessie's sympathy with the young girl and suggested that she should discourage it. Some years later, Chrissie wrote a book about her life. She had had a difficult time with drugs and alcohol and reached a turning point where her chances of survival were in question. With help, she turned her life around and went to college. The book related her time at Linton. She wrote how unfair she felt Mr. Sternwright had been to her. The one person she mentioned positively was Jessie who, she said, had helped her see that she was smart and could have a good future. Jessie said, "I had no idea that I had influenced Chrissie's life in any way." In her 80s, and active in her community, Jessie was still driving and traveling.

7 June 2003 was a perfect summer day for a group of 70 former Linton Camp School evacuees, their families, and four of their war-time teachers who gathered to picnic on Linton Village Green, Wharfedale, Yorkshire. The village green, with the whitewashed Fountain Arms standing beside it, the three gray stone bridges spanning the small beck flowing through the village, which, on that day, looked like a film set. We sat around the WWI memorial that stood to one side of the green opposite the Fountain Hospital, built by Richard Fountain, Esq., in the 1700s. He had made a fortune in London and left the sum of 26 pounds per annum, to be divided among six poor Linton men or women. He also left 20 pounds to a minister provided they read prayers twice in the week to the poor persons in the hospital.

Linton had changed little through the centuries, so it was not hard for any of us to remember this small village as it had been when we were evacuees. The Linton School was a half-a-mile walk from the village, and we walked there frequently to shop at the small village post office.

Mary Szpitter (Manley), a former student who remembered my brother, and her daughter worked to put on this celebration for Mr. Newbould's 90th birthday. The majority of these former evacuees, now in their 60s and 70s, had not seen their former schoolteachers, Mr. Frank Newbould, Mrs. Winifred Lowcock, Mrs. Jessie Robson, and Miss Ailsa Williams, since the early 1940s.

There were tears in the eyes of many of these stoic men and women as they greeted each other and remembered what, for some, had been some of the best years of their lives. With the arrival of 90 year-old Mr. Frank Newbould, their former coach, the "lads" from the former Linton Camp football team sang with a gusto that belied all their ages:

> Hurrah, Hurrah, for the boys in Green and Black
> Hurrah, Hurrah, for the boys in Green and Black
> Skipton was a very good team, but Linton was the best
> Hurrah, for the boys in green and black!

Later, at Linton Village Hall over tea and biscuits, memories were recalled of the school meal bell, the food, the "tapioca strike," the assemblies, the inspections, making beds with hospital corners, the clogs, canings, running away, and not least, the cold. One fellow remembered how his uncle, on his first visit to Linton, said he would never come again because it was so bitterly cold.

They fondly remembered the "silent" films, Laurel and Hardy, Keystone Cops, The Phantom of the Opera, and Charlie Chan. No one could forget the dancing. When the school opened on 10 July 1940, there were no books or pencils, but there was a radiogram and a few records. Everyone agreed that no evacuee, whatever sex or age, left Linton without being able to ballroom dance.

After Frank Newbould blew out the candles on his 90th birthday cake, he entertained the group with a powerful rendition of "Sargeant Major on Parade," his booming voice still powerful enough to impress and move all who heard it.

Wartime life on the Yorkshire Moors teaching evacuees had not been detrimental to his health. Nor to Miss Ailsa Williams, 90 in November 2003, who, the year before learned to use the computer and create original stationary. Mrs. Winifred Lowcock was still driving in her late 80s, and Mrs. Jessie Robson, also in her 80s, still traveled extensively.

Since that time, I have interviewed many of the former students and attended parties and re-unions with them. The information from former teachers and students was invaluable in providing me with a window into the Linton school, the staff and the day-to-day activities.

I remembered having been at a Methodist boy's school prior to going to Linton, but did not know where it was or why I was there. My mother refused to talk about this period of her life. Auntie Phyllis said she took me out for tea while I was at the school, but no one told me where it was. With no one around to question about the school's location, I set out to find out what I could learn.

In December 1997, I wrote to Ailsa, and described the boarding school I had attended prior to Linton. I explained that I had no idea where it was, but believed it to be at Apperley Bridge or Pateley Bridge. Ailsa researched the private schools in the area and, from my description of an old ivy-covered house with a Methodist church next door, told me she had located it. On a September day in 1998, she told me to come to her house in Ilkley and she would drive me to the school.

Ailsa insisted on driving her car and took me on a scenic tour of the area. We began with pastoral views, but the closer we came to Bradford the more industrial the surroundings became, even though the majority of woolen mills have been abandoned. Some of the mill buildings are now vibrant with new industries, as apartments, or art galleries. Ailsa drove straight to Apperley Bridge, to the Woodhouse Grove School, to the front door of the old, ivy-covered building. It looked exactly as it had the night I arrived there over fifty years before. Ailsa asked me if I wanted to go in. I shook my head, "No."

CHAPTER SIX

I t is January 1943. I'm standing at the gate of the Linton Residential Camp School for evacuee children in Yorkshire, England, feeling very sad and confused. I am five years old. Today mother brought me to the school to join my brother, Keith who has been here for six months. My mother is leaving me here separated from everything familiar to live, yet again, with strangers. Homesickness sweeps over me in waves, a feeling I will endure in various degrees throughout my life.

Other evacuee children surround us, some crying loudly as their parents, mainly mothers, hurry to the bus after their monthly two-hour visit. I hold tightly to my brother's hand, looking down at my new red clogs, an identity label pinned to my coat and my Mickey Mouse gasmask hung around my neck. Fighting back tears, I try to understand why mother will not take me home with her.

Mother explained before she left that Mr. Sternwhite, the headmaster, said he did not take children at the school under seven-years of age. She said, "Doreen, you have to be a good girl."

I ask myself, "If I am good at this school, will I get to go home?"

The cold wind blowing across the Yorkshire Moors reflects my misery as mother clasps me in her arms, her coat smelling of Evening-in-Paris. She said, "Be a good girl." Mother turns and hugs Keith, and hurries to the bus without looking back. I want to run after her and beg her to take me home with her.

Linton is the second boarding school I have been to. When my father went to the hospital mother said she had to work to earn money to feed us. She took a nursing job at the hospital where they took my father so she could be near him. "You and Keith have to go away to school," she explained, "We have no one in the family to take you."

I had no wish to return to the Methodist boy's school where Reverend Dean took me. Mother was formidable when it came to her children. Mother wanted to get me into the Linton School with my brother. She had managed to persuade Mr. Sternwhite to accept me. I knew she would be cross if I did something that meant I would have to leave.

As soon as mother's bus pulls away, Keith abruptly disappears to join the big boys. He is the only person I know here, and I want him to stay with me. I am afraid of everything. I am alone again, just as I was at the other school. Yet again, I am without my mother, father, and, it seems, my brother.

I wonder, "Was it something I did?"

I hold back the tears, experiencing a loss so great it renders me speechless. I don't cry. My body feels numb, as though some part of me has closed down. I feel an unfathomable ache, caused by a deep longing for the familiarity of home. "Oh, why doesn't mother take me home with her and tell me everything will be all right?" I freeze where I stand, unable to ask where I should go.

A pretty young woman with dark hair and a friendly smile approaches me. She asks my name and tells me she is Miss Hindle, the housemother for the small girls' dormitory. I do not answer. She checked the name on the label pinned to my coat.

Saying, "Come along, Doreen," she takes me by the hand and we walk, buffeted by the strong wind, down small cement paths, coming to a stop outside one of the dormitories, or huts, as Miss Hindle tells me the children call them. We enter a large, sparsely-furnished room with a bare wooden floor and twenty-five iron bunk beds with small lockers alongside them. Miss Hindle has a small cubicle at the end of the dormitory where she sleeps. In the corner of the large room is a Sani-lav with a small blue light over it. Miss Hindle says I can use it if I need to go to the toilet during the night. She asks if I understand. I do not answer. For the next two days, I speak to no one.

Miss Hindle explains that the real toilets are in the ablutions block and you have to go outside to use them. I am afraid of the dark, so I know I do not want to do that.

Miss Hindle said, "It's time for tea," so we put on our outdoor clothing to walk from one building to another. It was a cold walk to the dining-hall, where we sat on long, backless benches at long tables.

Before the meal the children said, "For what we are about to receive, may the Lord make us truly thankful." We had a cup of tea in a metal mug, with large slices of bread and butter - the children called them "doorsteps" - and jam. When the meal was finished, the children said, "For what we have received, may the Lord make us truly thankful."

After tea, Miss Hindle takes me to the classroom, where I will have lessons for an hour each evening.

That night, I lie in the bottom bunk, my heart heavy with incredible sadness. I say the prayers mother taught me before I sleep,

> Gentle Jesus, meek and mild, look upon a little child.
> God bless mother, father, Keith, Alan and everybody,
> through Jesus Christ our Lord, Amen.

Tonight I add a prayer of my own: "Please, God, let me go home."

Why did I have to come to another school to sleep yet again amongst strangers? I was helpless to do anything about my circumstances. I was sure that it was safer for me not to cry in public and to keep everything to myself. I tried to bury my thoughts deeply to protect myself from the pain that I did not want to feel.

Keith said he loved being at Linton because he didn't have to look after me. With a sick father, often in the hospital, and with mother having to work, Keith babysat me for many hours a day. At Linton, Keith had the freedom to play with his friends whenever he chose. All I wanted was to be at home with mother, father and my brother. Where was my father? Why hadn't mother or Keith mentioned him?

One of the first things I learned from the children at Linton was that my father had died.

On many nights, when the siren sounded, we children went out in the darkness to watch enemy aircraft as they flew on their deadly missions. One moonless evening we all rushed outside to see hundreds of German planes blanketing the sky overhead. They came over in never-ceasing waves – we had never before seen so many. They were going to bomb yet another British city and when they hit their targets, the sky lit up like a fireworks display. When the moon was full, the aircraft flew low enough that we could see the markings on them. Many of the older boys proudly showed off their knowledge as they identified the different *Luftwaffe* aircraft.

One evening, as the drone of the planes grew louder one of the older boys came over to me and said, "You're Keith's kid sister, aren't you?" I nodded. "Your father died. Keith went to the funeral," he told me. I didn't know what a funeral was. Nor did I really understand the word "died."

To this eleven-year-old boy, passing on this news was like relating the scores of the latest soccer match. He was almost happy to be conveying information that he had and I did not. He had no concept of the weight of his words. The boy knew what he knew because my brother had gone to my father's funeral. For the young man, it was nothing special. When he had passed on the information, he quickly turned his attention to the German bombers still droning past in the sky above. The older boys bet on the time it would take for German bombs to hit their targets. That was the interest of the moment.

The boys later told me that Stanley, the husband of my godmother, Vera, had died. The children said she awoke one morning and found her husband dead beside her. The army had rejected Stanley because of a bad heart condition, and a heart attack killed the twenty-two-year-old newlywed. The children did not know that Vera was only 19 years old and pregnant.

For a five year-old child, the world was a scary place, when, for entertainment, we evacuees watched enemy aircraft flying above our heads to wreak destruction on our cities, when the people you cared about abruptly disappeared from your life, when, yet again, you went away to live with strangers. Because no adult said anything about my father to me, I thought it a secret that only adults knew. Mother's intention was to protect me. She did not expect the children to tell me this news.

The headmaster had not said my father died, nor had my mother or brother. Because I heard from other children about my father's death, I believed that maybe it had not happened. I thought the boy who had told me could be wrong. My father was in the hospital – until I was told otherwise this was what I believed.

The description of Stanley dying beside Vera was an image that stayed with me for years. With no adult to explain, my imagination played the scene over and over. I shuddered to think about awakening and Stanley being dead beside Vera. Stanley was a kind man, who used to play with Keith and me whenever he visited Vera. We always had a lot of fun. Surely, someone would have explained if something had happened to him.

Although I tried to pretend what the boys said did not happen, I cried alone at night when no one could hear. I cried about the things I could not comprehend, for the life-changing events I was helpless to affect, and for an endless longing to have my family and life the way it was.

From that time on, I shut down the part of me that hurt. I did not trust people, particularly grown-ups. It was a mistrust I took into adulthood. I watched adults very carefully, trying to gain an under-standing of their intentions and moods. Can they be trusted and how will they treat me? I had no conception of what would happen and how long I would have to live at the school. Nothing in my world was certain. I buried my true feelings and showed only the "good girl" to what had become an increasingly frightening world.

Years later, at age eleven, I convinced myself that my "real" father would be there when I came home from school. For me he had never died; he had simply gone to the hospital. I decided that he had found us and went home with high hopes, which were crushed when he wasn't there.

Each child had to have a medical examination before acceptance at the school. This was something mum knew and I did not.

She took me to see a doctor in Bradford with hundreds of children in a large room with not even a screen for privacy. It was like an assembly line, each child called forward and examined by one doctor. I still remember him pulling down my panties, and, young as I was, how embarrassed I felt. I couldn't wait to leave. The clinic was in a hospital and as we left a nurse was displaying an Iron Lung outside the building. This was probably one of the first machines of its kind in the area and it was associated with polio patients. The nurse came and asked mother if her little girl "would like to try out the new machine." Mother was not pleased, and let the young woman know.

There was a basic clothing requirement for evacuated children. This made it prohibitive for some families to send their children away. Many families could afford to send only one child. Mother went shopping for the required clothing, which must have been hard to manage on her ten-shilling-a-week widow's pension.

I was both nervous and excited on the day I left for Linton because I so seldom went anywhere. Today, mum said, we were going on a Ribble coach, much fancier than the ordinary public transport buses.

The coach was standing outside the Alhambra Theatre when we arrived. Boarding it were mostly women going on their monthly visits to the school. I was the only child. We sank into the coach's comfortable seats and watched a group of black women standing across the street, some with babies in their arms and others with small children clinging to their skirts. "Mother, could we get a baby like that?" She smiled and told me how sad the baby's mother would be if it went to live with another family.

We drove through Bradford's streets. The back-to-back houses had lines full of washing that had frozen stiff on that cold January morning. At small shops, women queued for whatever the grocer or baker had for sale that day – oranges, sugar, or sometimes bread.

We saw some milkmen and coalmen, the few men to be seen on the streets not in military uniform. Usually, they were not fit or too old for military service. Young boys and girls with carts made from old pram wheels went on errands for their families. In wartime, making sure children went to school was not a high priority for poor parents. Some schools had shut their doors due to the evacuation of children. Mothers whose men had gone to fight the war considered their need of their children's help more important than their education.

Bradford's tall mill chimneys spewed black smoke and debris as the workers wove woolen material for military uniforms. The gray limestone mills and houses gave the city a dour look, reflected in the faces of people entrenched in the uncertainties of a country at war for four long years.

We passed the trams I loved to ride that shook and rattled along the track and the trolley buses that would glide along, with a low hum, on their overhead wires. Shortly, along with the tracks of the trams and trolleys, we left the city behind.

Suddenly, we were in the countryside and the scenery changed abruptly, from the mills and smoke of the city to the heather and rock formations of the moors.

Passing Yeadon aerodrome, I saw the largest silver balloon I had ever seen hovering about the ground. "What is that?" I asked. Mother explained, "It's a barrage balloon. They're used to prevent the Germans seeing and bombing the planes on the air-field. There are many of them around the country."

The coach wound its way up through the Pennines, the roads cut into gray rocks that towered above us. Hand-constructed gray walls snaked across every mile of the moor, keeping sheep from straying from farmers' fields.

Around one corner there stood a group of wild moor ponies. I had never seen these small sturdy animals before and wanted to pet them. "Look, Mum! Horses!" The animals, unkempt in their winter coats, stood on the bank, eyeing us with interest. After a moment, they abruptly kicked up their heels and bolted down the slope, their shaggy manes flying behind them as they disappeared from sight. The ponies looked like carefree and happy children. I longed to join them.

Every turn in the road brought a new scene of formations created by the ice age so many centuries before. Yorkshire women had grown up in industrial towns with an admiration for the moors and the coarse beauty that mirrored their own tough, blunt spoken independence. For most of these hardworking "folk" the moors were an escape from smoky cities, however briefly. It gave them a chance to picnic, fish, hike, or to dream of the possibilities. In 1943, for these women it was a brief respite from four years of war.

Each mile we drove made me more anxious. No one had explained that I would be staying at the school. I thought, or hoped, that we were going to visit Keith, who had been there since my father went to hospital. For some reason, no one had fully explained the situation, so I wasn't quite sure what to expect. I knew mother wanted me to go to the school with Keith, but I kept hoping to stay home with her.

Simon's Seat, a well-known formation of rocks, rose majestically in the distance as we passed through the picturesque villages of Grassington, Threshfield, and Linton. The houses, shops, walls and cobblestones were as gray as the sky.

A cold wind blew as we pulled into the school grounds. The entrance, through a barred wooden gate, looked neat and tidy, everything in its place. Linton was called a camp school and the buildings stood in neat rows as though conforming to military commands. Mother said Mr. Sternwhite, who had served in the Navy in WWI, ran the school with military precision.

The school had a red Royal Letter Box, built into the wall at the entrance. I was impressed that the school had its own letterbox. Keith met us as we got of the coach. We walked past the school clinic just beyond the entrance, down a slight slope, and then climbed a long flight of stairs to Mr. Sternwhite's office. Keith said he would wait outside.

Mr. Sternwhite's demeanor matched his name, but everyone said his bark was worse than his bite. I certainly hoped it was if I had to stay at Linton. I knew I did not want to go back to cold baths, morning runs and half a chipolata sausage. Mr. Sternwhite was smoking a pipe and stood up when we entered. He offered us chairs in front of his desk. He knew of mother's situation, because he had told Keith of my father's death and arranged his journey to Bradford to attend the funeral.

Mr. Sternwhite shook my hand and said, "We don't usually take children under seven. Those are the rules. But because your brother is here, I have agreed to let you come to the school." He added, "You have to promise to be a good girl." Mother spoke for me and assured him I would be good. I knew I would have to be good, but kept hoping he would not let me come to join Keith at the school. Mother and I went back down the steep office steps and met Keith.

Keith was anxious to walk to the village of Linton. The children could only leave school grounds with a teacher or parent. The three of us walked the half-mile into Linton village with its houses, bridges and Fountaine hospital, an almshouse left by a landowner hundreds of year before. It all looked gray and forbidding to a small girl on that cold afternoon. The light was on in the village shop, the only welcoming sign. We bought some powdered milk, each of us licking our fingers, pretending it was the lemonade powder. We walked over each of the village's three bridges. We collected sticks and threw them into the water as the ducks swam towards us, looking for food.

There were several large, imposing houses in the village, but my favorite was the one with stepping-stones across a small stream leading from the road to the house.

As we walked back to the school, a young, pregnant woman came along the road towards us. As we passed her, much to my Mother's embarrassment, my brother said in a very loud voice, "Oh, mother, hasn't that lady had a big dinner?"

Back at the school, we had a cup of tea in the dining room before it was time for mother to leave. I clung to my mother's hand as we walked together to the coach that stood outside the school entrance. I knew I had to be good or they would not let me stay. Keith disappeared as soon as the coach left, anxious to re-join his friends.

We had assembly each morning, when the entire school and the teachers met. One of the teachers said a prayer and talked about things related to the day ahead. Classes were held in the mornings and again after tea. In the afternoons, we could go for nature walks, on picnics, play games, or learn country dancing. The Girl Guide and Boy Scout troops had their meetings.

One cold winter afternoon, the snow was deep on the ground, so we went to the top field to build snowmen. We girls managed to make a snowman, but we didn't stay long outside when our wool gloves proved no match for the wet snow and the bitter cold winds. Some of the boys cut the snow into blocks and tried to make an igloo that became a great source of pleasure for all the children.

In the top field we pulled the sledge up to the top of the hill, and I went down the hill with a bigger girl. It was scary, but fun – and cold. Unfortunately, there were few sledges and many children so the trips were limited. Mother had bought me red clogs similar to those many of the other children wore. The clogs had metal and wooden slats shaped like wish bones underneath. With each step, snow packed under the soles. I became taller each time I moved and eventually lost my balance. I spent a lot of time falling down and attempting to clear the snow from my clogs with my woolen gloves. The clogs were like shoes and did not protect the legs, so my legs and fingers quickly became frozen. I walked back to the hut that afternoon soaking wet and very cold. The big boys didn't seem to mind the cold and were the only ones still sliding down the hill when the light began to fade.

I also remember a warm summer afternoon when Miss Williams took us small girls on a picnic. We crossed the road and climbed over the wall opposite the school, running and tumbling down the hill to the bank opposite Linton Church. Miss Williams let us paddle in the River Wharfe, as it flowed gently over the rocks and past the church. We loved to walk across the stepping-stones to the Church, which was without the usual steeple, but instead featured a squat bump on top.

In most English villages, the church is built next to the pub. Linton Church of Angels and St. Michael is on the bend of the River Wharfe quite a distance from the villages it served: Linton, Threshfield, Grass-ington and, at one time, Hebden. Because it was built on the curve of the river it was said to have originally been a pagan church.

Whatever kind of church it was, we children loved to paddle in the river and play on its grassy banks. The church was less than a quarter of a mile down the slope from the school.

We enjoyed the picnic lunch and after we had eaten, we gathered around Miss Williams on the grass. She read to us from Charles King-sley's *The Water Babies,* explaining that the author used to stay in the Dales and had written this story when he had visited friends who owned a home close by. I loved to hear about Tom, the little boy who swept chimneys. I felt sorry for him and wondered why people would allow their children to do such awful work. It must have been scary for Tom, lowered into those huge chimneys and their sooty depths. How did he breathe? And did he ever have a bath and look clean? He always looked dirty in the pictures we were shown.

It was an unusually hot afternoon. Eventually, I fell asleep.

Mr. Newbould, my brother's housemaster, was in charge of the toys and clothing received from what they called The American Foundation.

One of my most wonderful memories of Linton was receiving a Raggedy Anne Doll and a Raggedy Anne and Andy Book. They were prized possessions for many years. The people who sent these wonderful gifts also wrote letters to me. Unfortunately, the government censored every letter from abroad before we received it. Names and addresses, and any information that could identify where they lived or who they were had been removed or blacked out. We were never able to thank the people who were so kind to us.

Mr. Newbould was also the keeper of the Tuck Shop. All the children's sweet coupons were combined to allow the school to buy sweets in bulk. A special day of the week was chosen for us to visit the Tuck Shop. What a wonderful time we had deciding which sweets to buy. Every child looked forward to the visit – the bright spot in the week and a happy time for all.

Nurse O'Connor was popular with both students and staff. A gregarious Irish woman with red hair, she charmed everyone who came her way. The older boys said all the male teachers flirted with her. I was not sure what that meant, but I liked her a lot. We wondered how many of the students were conveniently ill in order to receive the extra attention she provided.

Because of the scarcity of food, the Ministry of Food allocated certain items for British children to supplement their diets. Every day we queued outside the clinic to receive, from a huge tin container, a tablespoonful of malt and cod-liver oil. The government provided the brown-colored substance, which was thick like molasses, but tasted much better. In fact, in time we became used to the taste and considered it a treat. We also received government-issued condensed orange juice, which had to be diluted with water. At our break each morning, every child received a small bottle of milk.

We began each day with a wake-up at 7:45 a.m. Regardless of the weather, we went to the girl's ablutions block, across the street from our dormitory, to wash. Returning to the dormitory, we had to strip the beds and put the bedding into a bed bag. The teachers expected us children to keep the dormitories tidy. This was not difficult because there was so little furniture and no rugs on the wooden floors.

The dining room was in another building, and we gathered there each morning for a breakfast of cornflakes, watery powdered eggs, or porridge so stiff you could stand a spoon up in it.

From the dining room, we went to the assembly hall where each morning at 9:30 a.m., the whole school, students, teachers, and staff, gathered. From there we went to morning classes.

Lunch was at 12:00 p.m., and cooking with limited wartime resources proved challenging for the kitchen staff. Often the school could not get meat, so we ate a lot of Spam, and a great deal of watery cabbage.

One lunchtime, we had figs and custard for dessert. I could not swallow the figs. The teacher asked why I was not eating and I said, "I don't like figs." She told me to eat them. I refused. She made me sit at the table from lunch until teatime. I did not eat the figs. I fell asleep with my arms on the table.

She would not allow me to have tea, so I sat looking at those figs until the meal was over. That incident stuck in my mind, and I have never eaten a fig from that day to this. I often wondered why we began and ended each meal being truly thankful for the food we ate, when often it was so awful.

One afternoon, we small girls were playing in the assembly hall, all of us running up onto the stage and jumping off. Suddenly, when I jumped from the stage a teacher grabbed hold of me and slapped my legs. I cried both with shock and from the pain of her hitting me. Some of the older boys must have seen the incident and told my brother, Keith. A few minutes later, I saw my brother burst through the door looking very angry. He ran to the teacher and started hitting her. I was pleased that Keith came to my support. I have no memory of what happened next. Mr. Sternwhite did not allow the teachers to slap children. The children received the cane as punishment, but it was something they were told about. It was not used in the heat of the moment.

The teachers and staff at Linton Residential School did the best they could for the children with the resources they had. In many cases, the Linton children were better off than those sent to live with families they did not know. While many of those children were well treated, others went to families who used them to work in the house, or on the land to replace male workers who had gone to war. A number of evacuees were even abused physically and sexually.

Linton initially had approximately 240 children who came from various schools and orphanages around Yorkshire. When the Germans threatened to occupy The Channel Island, the British government sent a ship to evacuate the children. Two families of three boys came to Linton from their homes in the Channel Islands. One sad young Jewish boy and his sister left behind their family in Dusseldorf and came to England. The host family sent the sister to Bradford Grammar school and her brother to Linton. It must have been so difficult for these children not to know anything about the welfare of the families they left behind.

Writing this book has been one of the hardest things I have ever done. For years, I have attempted to complete this story but have always found an excuse not to finish. The truth is that writing about such a childhood is painful. You have to relive the time, and events, and to remember people who once were an important part of your life. People who, in most instances, are no longer with us.

Writing about events makes them concrete. They become real and with that reality, it is sometimes possible to put that period of your life to rest. For decades, I had little knowledge about those early years, except for brief, exceptionally vivid memories.

Today, as someone recently observed, we would have had two counselors for each evacuee child, helping them to deal with the events of their evacuation. There were no counselors for the evacuees. After the fact, the evacuees were told to forget what had happened. Life had to go on. The war was over.

For many evacuees, the war was not over and, not able to deal with their past, it was difficult for them to move forward to the future. We all understand that a house needs a good foundation, and the same applies to people. When the foundation is not solid, and negative issues not addressed, children have difficulty surviving, let alone enjoying their lives. The British government felt no obligation to provide support for the children it sent away. The evacuees were repeatedly told that they should simply forget their experiences -- the war was over.

Through the years, I have met many WW II evacuees, and whether they had positive or negative experiences, most agree that the evacuation changed their lives.

The degree to which it affected them varied with each individual and each experience. Some still resent the fact that their parents sent them away and maybe not a brother or a sister. In numerous cases, the bond between parents and children was broken, or significantly changed by the experience. After all these years, many former evacuees still ask one question: "Why did they send me away?"

If this narrative helps just one person have a clearer understanding of what happened to them so many years ago, the effort will have been worth it. Childhoods were lost, and childhoods *do* matter.

CHAPTER SEVEN

◇◇

O n an autumn day in 1999, Rose Goy (Bowers), met with Mary Manley (Szpitter) and Dorothy North in a Bradford restaurant to make a tape for me about their Linton experiences.

Rose Goy said she was on one of the first coaches from Bradford to arrive at Linton Residential School on 10 July 1940. Rose was a small, fair-haired, quiet nine-year-old. She would be age fourteen before she left the school in January 1945.

Mary Manley went to Linton in September 1940, two months after Rose. Her parents initially refused to let her go to the countryside "out of harm's way." The night a bomb fell on St. Peter's Church, Leeds Road, Bradford, a site that was close to their home, Mary's parents changed their minds. The next morning Mary went with her grandfather to see the damage to the church and the crater the bomb had made. After the bomb dropped, Mary's parents arranged for her to be evacuated.

Dorothy North went to Linton from her grandmother's home where she lived with her mother. Although evacuation was voluntary if a household had a spare bedroom, the authorities could insist on them taking in a soldier or an evacuee. When Dorothy's father joined the army, Dorothy and her mother went to live with her grandparents to fill their spare bedroom. Her grandparents thought they were too old to take in strangers.

Rose and Mary had been "best friends," at Linton, and kept in touch throughout the years. With a down to earth wisdom that belied her years, Mary was a little older than Rose was. In school photographs, Mary has dark hair cut to shoulder length sometimes with a bow on one side. By her own admission, her years at Linton made her independent something her parents had a hard time coming to terms with when she left the school.

Jessie remarked in 2008, "Mary was very responsible - I can see her now on the path leading from the clinic where she often helped Nurse O'Connor with the younger children. Mary loved working with the little ones and spent hours taking care of them. The staff needed all the help they could get. Children, like Mary, were given responsibility, because the staff needed the help – "we were always shorthanded in the first few years," said Jessie. Mary helped the nurse give Malt and Cod-Liver Oil to the children each day. After the children became used to the taste they considered it a treat and, "I used to give a little extra to my friends," Mary said.

Nurse O'Connor put Rose in quarantine at the clinic when she got measles. "She did not want the illness spread throughout the school," Rose explained. She remembered how completely alone she was during that time. "No one could visit me. They left my meals outside the door. It was a very lonely time," Rose said. While Rose may have suffered, the measles did not spread to the rest of the school.

I spoke with Dorothy North at a Christmas party at Mary Manley's home in 2000 and she said how homesick she had been at Linton. Dorothy took and passed the Scholarship exam and left Linton after being there for only about eighteen months. She said, "When I think back to that time, it probably was better than I thought, but I hated being away from my family and never settled down. I am still friends with Mary and Rose but after Linton, I did not remain in one place long enough to make friends. My mother moved so often. I attended seven different schools."

All three said the Linton boys and the girls did not mix very much. While they remembered the names of many of the girls, they could recall few of the boy's names. However, all three did remember my brother Keith. Mary said it was because "Keith was good at sports and played on the soccer and cricket teams." Dorothy agreed, "The boys who played sports were more likely to be the ones I remembered. I knew the girls so much better." Rose said, "Keith was fair-haired and quiet." Jessie told me, "Keith didn't say very much. He was well behaved and always well dressed. I can see his face as though he was standing in front of me right now."

The Linton school day began with the Head Boy, who Mary said, "Would walk up and down the path outside the dormitories at 7:45 am each morning, ringing the bell to wake us up. Do you remember it was a big triangle and he struck it repeatedly? It made such a racket. It certainly woke us all up. Then the first thing we had to do was go out every morning, whatever the weather, to the ablutions block to wash. It was awful. When it was cold it felt like punishment".

The ablutions block had communal showers, which at that time was quite unusual. "I had never seen a shower before" Dorothy recalled,

"There was a row of wash basins opposite. And a slipper bath, but only one and you had to put your name on a list to use it."

The children all had their towels numbered to correspond with hooks that had the same number. Mary recalled that the toilet paper had nursery rhymes printed on it, but she said, "It was still stiff hard paper." She laughed and said, "Even so, it was better than at home – our family used torn newspaper."

They all spoke of Miss Hammond, the girl's physical education teacher, and Miss Dickinson who said they were, "sporty ladies" who wore divided skirts, "what we would call culottes today. They were ahead of their time," Mary said. Rose added, "Do you remember Miss Hammond would turn the showers cold and make us run through them when she was on duty."

Mr. Newbould told me how some of the older girls brought bathing costumes to Linton. "We didn't have a swimming pool," he said. "They wore the suits in the showers and the teachers could not get the girls to remove them."

When they left the ablution block, they walked back to the dormitories and finished dressing. All the children regardless of age had to make their beds and tidy the dormitory. The dormitories only had the iron bunk beds with a small open container that stood between the beds divided into four compartments. Four children shared the space. Fortunately, Mary said, "We didn't have many clothes or belongings."

Mr. Sternwhite had served in the British Navy in World War I and ran the school Navy style – the only way he knew. He made the rules, which both the staff and the children followed. The teachers agreed it was easier to manage the children when everything was shipshape.

For children unused to tidying their rooms it must have come as a shock to live by Mr. Sternwhite's rules. The sheets could be converted into a bag and the children put their blankets into it and placed it at the end of the bed. The children made their beds each evening with hospital corners – each one as neat as the next. If children left their shoes in the room, they had to place them at the end of the bed facing the same way.

According to Mr. Newbould, when Mr. Sternwhite first saw the gray blankets allocated for the children, he became irate. "These thin blankets can't keep anyone warm, especially in the winter on these moors," he complained. No one believes he got the blankets replaced. However, each child did receive two blankets in winter. I can vouch for the fact that they did not keep us very warm.

With the beds made, the children walked to the dining-hall for breakfast.

Dorothy reflected that, "Linton had what the staff referred to as this wonderful fresh air. All the buildings in Bradford were black, covered in soot from the mill chimneys. I suppose the air must have been as dirty as the buildings. Despite the harsh weather, it must have been much better for us than all that sooty Bradford air. However, at the time, I did not appreciate that 'fresh air' which often was cold enough to freeze a brass monkey. However, with all the walking we did we must have been fit."

Mary recalled one year they had an exceptional amount of snowfall and, "We were unable to use the front door of the dormitories, because they were blocked with huge snowdrifts. Fortunately, we had a side door that we could use. The moors were so open there was nothing to stop the wind and we frequently had drifts higher than the stone walls."

The breakfast bell rang and the children gathered at the dining hall. We seated ourselves at the long tables on backless benches and one of the staff blew a whistle for us to be quiet. Rose remembered, "We said grace before being allowed to eat. Then we repeated the grace with the variation of 'being thankful for we had received,' before we left the table." We all queued and took a plate, and filled it with whatever was for breakfast.

There was always a big tin saucepan containing porridge that Dorothy said, "tasted like wallpaper paste, and a tin tray of thickly cut toast." Unfortunately, wartime bread, baked with unrefined flour, had a gray-beige, unappetizing color and a similar taste.

Mention of the toast reminded Dorothy, "The school used Nelson's Marmalade, huge tins of it – the cheapest you could get. It was always runny and people said that the raspberry pips were made of wood. Maybe it just tasted that way. We always drank tea or cocoa from tin mugs. For some reason we had fried bread every morning, occasionally with sausages, which didn't taste like the sausages we had at home – goodness knows what they were made from. We never saw a real egg. We had big tins of scrambled eggs made from powdered egg – they were really watery. Ugh! However unpleasant it looked we either ate it or went hungry."

They all spoke of the main meal of the day served at lunchtime that often included some form of meat. Spam, shepherd's pie, minced beef and carrots and cabbage, boiled until it was almost unrecognizable.

The puddings varied little – Sago, semolina, prunes and custard, and jam or treacle sponge, the latter made with suet, which resulted in a greasy, leaden lump. There was also the ever-present tapioca. Teddy

Tong told me, "We were served tapioca so many times we went on a 'Tapioca Strike.' We simply refused to eat it anymore."

Dorothy said one of the worst evening meals was, "thin soup and ship's biscuits that were as hard as bricks and tasted like sawdust. We hated them."

Ailsa had an interesting observation about the cook, who, she said, "made a lot of inedible food for the staff and children. However, if visitors came to the school to eat, he could do a very good job and put on a 'wonderful meal.'"

In retrospect, the three women realized that it must have been difficult for the kitchen staff to prepare tasty and nutritious meals for the children with rationing and food shortages. "We must have given up our ration books to the school for them to buy in bulk. The problem was the catering staff had so little choice of food items," said Dorothy.

Frank Newbould told me "The meals were quite good - to say it was wartime, the children ate well." It should be said that Mr. Newbould was called up to serve in the army from 1941–1942 and later from 1944-1945. He may have found the Linton meals more to his liking than British army food.

Mary, Rose and Dorothy agreed the children of today would not appreciate those wartime meals.

What the children did not understand was how, at times during the war, the food shortages were severe.

The British food shortages became so bad that shops that sold horsemeat for animals prior to the war now sold it for human consumption. In 1943, newspapers and magazine articles, encouraged people to buy horsemeat which, one article said, 'was very tasty especially in steak and kidney pie.'[19] The next suggestion for the British menu was whale meat. British housewives tried it in many guises but rejected it as 'terrible,' 'awful,' 'too salty,' or 'too fishy tasting.'"

With fewer ships available to transport goods, Jennifer Davies reported, "Some of the meat was dehydrated; other meat had the bones taken out – in fact in the latter case housewives sometimes found it difficult to identify the anonymous lump they were looking at. By 1944, this 'putting food into battle dress,' as one food official termed it, had saved the carrying capacity of seventy-five 10,000 ton ships."[20]

In the event that "enemy blockades" reduced the country to starvation levels, a nutritionist suggested eating hedgehogs, badgers, muskrats and snakes. A professor, obviously believing that you should practice what you preach, had a foot of zoo python boiled for himself. "He ate it for lunch with potato chips, but came to the considered opinion that it was indistinguishable from boiled string." [21]

Sausages that looked plump when bought contained so little meat they cooked down to a point were they were hard to see on the plate. A little known fact is that meat in Britain stayed on ration until June 1954.

The British Minister of Food, Lord Woolton, encouraged the public throughout the war, "To eat potatoes instead of bread," a phrase used regularly on cooking programs, because it saved the shipping of wheat. Film, Radio, newspapers and Government pamphlets inundated the public with "Food Flashes" and cookery advice, *ad nauseam*. This was one of many jingles played on the radio each morning before the program Kitchen Front:

Those who have the will to win
Cook potatoes in their skin
Knowing that the sight of peelings
Deeply hurts Lord Woolton's feelings. [22]

Spam was also a constant on the school menu. In addition, while initially it tasted better than some other meats we did eat a lot of it. Wartime comedians frequently joked about Spam. One of the jokes was about a Sunday afternoon, at Hyde Park's, Speakers' Corner in London where a man shouted to his audience, "Why are we fighting this War?" The answer came from a lone cockney voice in the crowd who replied, "For Spam."

The Linton children did not know or probably care that the catering staff were facing such difficulties obtaining food. The children knew they disliked the watery eggs, watery cabbage, potatoes, soup and ships' biscuits and having tapioca at almost every meal. They complained that almost nothing "tasted good." Unfortunately, they had to eat the food because with the exception of fish and chips in Grassington on Friday nights there was nowhere else for the children to buy food.

The women remembered that their parents, coming to visit, always brought something special. Bread and confectionary items required coupons so their parents must have sacrificed so that the children could have a monthy treat.

Mary said, "Do you remember we would go scrumping for apples and when you had finished eating an apple some of the boys would ask for the cores? I always wondered why because we had eaten all the fruit and little remained. I suppose at times we all must have been really hungry."

The children planted a victory garden that Mary said, Was just opposite the big girl's dorm. "I remember we would 'pinch' the peas when they were ready. We also used to eat raw carrots and turnips." She thought a moment and said, "Do you know we thought they were a treat?"

Mrs. Carter at the Linton village Post Office would sometimes have khali or lemon sugar powder to sell. Mr. Reg Bonus, at the small grocer's shop might have a large sack full of liquorice roots, which Yorkshire people called, 'Spanish.' We children would walk the half mile to Linton to buy a couple of Spanish roots for a penny and suck on them until the taste had gone. Mary said she put the roots in the bottom of a large jug and poured boiling water on them to make a liquorice drink.

Like all British schoolchildren, the Linton evacuees collected rose hips plentiful when the wild-rose blooms faded. The Women's Voluntary Association and the Women's Institutes countrywide enlisted the help of all British schoolchildren. The Rosehips were an excellent source of vitamin C and British manufacturers turned them into syrup.

Mr. Davidson was the camp manager, who took care of the running of the school buildings. He also ran the tuck-shop when Mr. Newbould was away. These former evacuees remember that he would open the shop just one day a week on Fridays. They said how patient he was with the boys who got bored while waiting and started to fight or cause trouble. Each child had the opportunity to choose something from the sweets available, as long as they had enough coupons and pocket money. During wartime, there was a drastic cut in the choice of items such as chocolates, sweets and biscuits. We children were pleased with anything that broke the monotony of our diets. The decision of what to chose was difficult; Dolly Mixtures, Sherbert Dips, gob-stoppers, Fox's mints, Maltesers, Jelly Babies, Fry's, Terry's and Cadbury's chocolates, and the penny tray where the cheaper sweets were displayed. That Friday visit to the Tuck-Shop was the highlight of our week.

We had assemblies in the morning where we sang a couple of hymns and one of the teachers read a prayer. Of course, the Church of England (or "C of E") was the state church, and the country's main religion. The Lincolnshire-born Charles Wesley, however, worked his way around Wales and the North of England, including the Yorkshire Dales. He left behind a great many Methodist (or Wesleyan) churches and "chapel folk" in the area.

Nurse O'Connor and Mary were Roman Catholics and most Sundays went to the services at the Linton Church. On rare occasions, they cycled the ten miles to Skipton, to attend the nearest Catholic Church. Mary said she was saddle-sore each time they made the trip, and when she reached the quarry, a few miles from the school, she would get off her bike and push it up the hills to Linton. Children from other religions would not have had a place to worship.

The afternoons were free for the varied extra curricular activities. Mary remembered that the Girl Guides met in Grassington and some of the girls joined just to get away from the school. On Friday nights, the older children went to the pictures in Grassington and if they had the money, bought fish and chips from a van that parked in Grassington square. Mary said, "We looked forward to those fish and chips all week."

According to Mr. Newbould, the staff took it in turns to escort the children from Linton to Grassington and back. In the winter, especially on moonless nights, it was hard to see your way. With no road signs, even the local people became confused on those dark nights.

Many Yorkshire tales told about the moors being alive after dark, with ghosts, elves and haunted hounds. The children knew about Pam the Fiddler, a local ghost who, the locals believed, played in the Threshfield School at night. Ella Pontefract in her book *Wharfedale* wrote, "Old Pam is something of a fairy ghost. Occasionally at night, the windows of the school light up, and then you know that Pam is holding his school there. People who have dared to peep in at the windows at this time claim to have seen him fiddling to his scholars. There are people today who would not pass Threshfield School alone in the dark."[23]

While the children may have loved this and the many other tales in the light of day, the images made them nervous on their weekly walk past the Threshfield School on their way to Linton. Mr. Newbould said, "Mary would often come and hold my hand as we walked back."

On Saturday and Sunday afternoons, the children wrote letters to their parents. On Sunday nights, Mr. Oxley brought films, The Keystone Cops, Laurel and Hardy, Charlie Chaplin, Phantom of the Opera, and other silent films. The films the children occasionally saw at the Grassington Town Hall were more up-to-date.

Many times during the day, the staff put the records on the radiogram for dancing. Jessie said the radiogram was a blessing and remembered the three records left with it when the school opened: *I'll Be With You In Apple Blossom Time; One Dozen Roses; We Met at the Stage Door*. She said, "We played them over and over again; it's a wonder they didn't wear out. It seems odd now but the gramophone needles were so important; we could not afford to lose or break them."

Jessie said all the children could dance because, to fill any spare time, between mealtimes or lessons, they would put on the music and dance. She said, "Even I learned to dance at Linton: the foxtrot, the quick step, the Valetta, and the Gay Gordons. Arthur Firth was a fourteen-year-old student who taught me to waltz." She repeated the phrase I heard from teachers and students alike, "There wasn't one child who left Linton who could not dance."

Mr. Newbould agreed but had another perspective when he said, "It was another way to keep the children occupied and out of trouble."

Many of the staff came from families where they gathered around the piano and sang. Several of the staff members could play the piano: Mr. Newbould, Mr. (Pop) Essem and Jessie Suttle. On winter evenings they would sing songs that ran the gamut from rousing hymns – *Jerusalem* and *Onward Christian Soldiers* – to the wartime favorites *Run Rabbit Run*, *Hang out the Washing on the Siegfried Line*, *Lily Marlene* and *White Cliffs of Dover*. A special favorite, the chorus of the Yorkshire song, C.W. Murphy and Dan Lipton's, *My Girl's a Yorkshire Girl* used by James Joyce in his novel *Ulysses*:

> *My Girl's a Yorkshire Girl*
> *Yorkshire Through and Through*
> *My Girl's a Yorkshire Girl*
> *Eh! By gum, she's a champion!*
> *Though she's a factory lass*
> *And wears no fancy clothes,*
> *Still I've a sort of a Yorkshire relish*
> *For my little Yorkshire Rose*

No Yorkshire singsong was complete without the "Yorkshire National Anthem," *On Ilkla' Moor Bhar T'*at (On Ilkley Moor Without a Hat) always sung with great gusto.

With no money to buy toys, the youngsters entertained themselves playing Kick the Can, Tin Can Squat, Cock of the Midden, Hopscotch and at Easter time the girls played whip and tops. The boys built dens in the Top fields. Much to the farmer's dismay sometimes the children hopped over the wall to Bolton Hill where there were Iron Age ruins in the surrounding areas and the farmer thought the children might damage one of these ancient sites.

The evacuees made their own sledges, kites, and slingshots and they collected chestnuts from the enormous trees. The children put holes through the nuts and threaded string through them. The objective was to destroy the other person's 'conker' by aiming your conker at the one held by the other person.

With a cotton bobbin and four nails, the children created colorful strings from odd scraps of wool. In the winter, they picked bare branches from the trees and decorated them with colored wax to look like flowers. The children were pleased to work with anything to brighten a world of black cars, black curtains and drab clothes with few splashes of color.

Dormitory three was the Housecraft block one-half equipped for woodworking and shoe repair. The boys were the majority students for the classes.

Fred Walton taught the children to repair shoes and didn't mind if the girls wanted to learn also. Mary remembered that for their Girl Guide badges she and Rose had each repaired a pair of shoes. Evidently,

Mary did such an excellent job Mr. Walton took her shoes around to all the Bradford schools to show the boys what a good job a girl had done.

Rose laughed when she told us about her favorite shoe repair story. "I hit my finger with a hammer and my friend Sheila said, 'did it hurt.' I said to Sheila, Put your finger there, and she did. I brought the hammer down on her finger and said 'did it hurt.'" Jessie Robson remembered this incident and said the teachers could not believe that Rose, who was such a quiet child, had actually done such a thing. "Sheila was really hurt and had to go to the Nurse," said Jessie.

Both boys and girls took house crafts. The aim of the housekeeping course was to teach the basics of washing and cookery. All three women remembered having cooking lessons with Miss Nicholson and Miss Wilman. As their skills improved, they cooked a meal for the staff. With so little food choices, they had to be quite creative. One of their most exotic menus was Irish stew, sometimes without the lamb. Mary said, "We had three cookers and we did everything from setting the table to serving the meal. We really enjoyed ourselves and the food was better than school food."

Mr. Dunn taught woodwork for the boys and the girls. Mary said she gave her parents some bookends she had carved and "They had them for years." When visiting with Mr. Newbould in the late 1990s he showed me a pipe and a letter holder that some of the Linton boys had made in woodwork class in 1941. He had kept and used them for over fifty years.

Teddy Tong spoke of the money he made darning socks. A strong indication of how the wartime generation, even the children, learned to preserve and reuse all items of clothing. Most Yorkshire children would have had hand knitted socks because that was the cheapest way to obtain them. The parents went to the mill, bought the wool without coupons, and knitted jumpers, cardigan and socks.

The children learned to darn their socks because it took money and coupons, both in short supply, to buy them, and financially out of reach for most Linton parents. Shoe repair was also a saving for parents who could not afford to buy new shoes as often as needed. In the 60th Anniversary copy of *The Evacuee*, there is a picture of Kennylands, another school built by the National Camps Corporations. The picture shows a group of boys darning socks. An image we would never see in today's throwaway society.

All the girls, and some boys, learned to knit. Because of the numbers of sheep raised on the moors, most of the dales people, men and women learned to knit at very young ages. Wool, easily obtained from the local Bradford mills, even during the war. The nearby village of Dent was the village of knitters, so it seemed natural that the children would learn. As all three former Linton students' said, "Most of my jumpers and socks were knitted by my mother."

During walks on the moors, the older children learned to identify the different heathers, birds, and indigenous plants. They learned to have respect, for the iron-age sites, the wild ponies and other moor creatures.

The women remembered the fields in spring and summer, when the woods around Linton were full of bluebells, primroses, snowdrops and crocuses and the Sandoval flowers that grew only where the soil contained lead. Their appreciation for plants and for the beauty of the moors, to which they frequently return, is something all agreed they learned during their time at Linton. These three women were among many of us who feel drawn and have returned repeatedly to the area.

A local song written by Willie Foster of Beckermonds, includes the following two lines that speaks to the love of Wharfedale by these normally taciturn Yorkshire folk.

> Beautiful Wharfedale, so sweet and so fair
> Nowhere in England can with thee compare. [24]

While people from other parts of the country would counter their claim, it is an indication of the strong feelings local people had for the dales.

Teddy Tong summed up his days at Linton when he said, "We always had friends to play with – we evacuees were never bored."

At a Bradford Council meeting in May 1940, Council member Kathleen Chambers, who in 1945 became Bradford's first female Lord Mayor, discussed how she had seen evacuee children from the city who were without adequate clothing. She felt it was "a shame" that mothers, whose husbands were serving in the war, were unable to find the money, to buy suitable footwear and clothing for their children. Councilor Chambers said, "I felt ashamed Bradford did not look after their children better than that."

While the majority of children at Linton came from the Bradford area, some came from further afield. In 1940 when the Germans occupied France it was just a matter of time before they also occupied the Channel Islands. The British government sent a ship to take the children off the islands prior to the German occupation. There were three boys called Cleels, and three boys called Gallienne, who came to the school from the Channel Islands.

In a 2008 interview, Jessie told me the names of the Gallienne brothers, Edmund, Raymond and David. When they arrived in Bradford, they lived with a doctor and his wife on Manningham Lane, a very upscale area of Bradford at the time. For some reason, the boys who Jessie says were probably from about nine to twelve-years-old, later went to Linton. Jessie recalls taking a bicycle ride one summer evening with another member of staff and Edmund Gallienne. She said, "I remember because he had a bicycle and not many of the children did."

According to Ailsa, "The Cleels were little demons." When we consider the changes these children had gone through it would have been surprising if they had not been. Abruptly taken from their parents and the island where they knew everyone had to be heart breaking and a huge cultural shock for children who possibly did not speak English as a first language.

The name that both teachers and students mentioned was a young, Jewish German boy called Kurt Asch. According to Winifred, "His father had been a judge in Dusseldorf, Germany and he sent Kurt and his sister for safety to a wool merchant friend in Bradford. They sent the girl to Bradford Grammar School, a day school. Kurt they sent to Linton. Winifred said, "Can you imagine what a shock it must have been for that young man who had come from a comfortable home to be boarding at Linton. He did not speak a great deal of English and the fact that he was German made him the target of the other children. He had a very difficult time."

Winifred told the story of how one day the Birdsall Jeweler in Skipton rang Mr. Sternwhite to say that a young man had tried to "flog" the silver plate that the jeweler recognized was from the Linton Church. She said, "It didn't really surprise us when it was Kurt who broke into the Linton Church and stole the church silver. The staff realized just how unhappy this young man must have been. Obviously, he did not know of any other way of getting back to his family." The most revealing part of this episode for me was the fact that although each member of the staff remembered the incident in explicit detail, none of the former students had heard of it.

I believe Mr. Sternwhite kept the information from the children in order to protect Kurt. I thought that spoke a lot about the sensitivity of the headmaster many thought to be stern and harsh. Kurt simply disappeared from the school. None of the children knew why he had left.

Winifred said, "Many years later, a very smart young man appeared at the Nurse's office and said in a strong American accent, "Do you remember me? My name is Kurt Asch. He told Nurse O'Connor and Winifred he lived in the United States and owned a chain of restaurants in California.

I have made extensive enquiries about Kurt but have been unable to trace him. I believe he would be pleased to hear how fondly the staff and pupils remembered him. In hindsight, how they recognized the intense difficulties he, as a young boy of no more than 12 years of age had faced. Living in another country separated from his parents he was old enough to know how the Nazis treated Jewish families. His sister came each visiting day – she lived in Bradford and him at Linton. The distance was only thirty miles, but it must have seemed like a much greater distance. How fearful and confused this young child must have been.

In defense of the teachers, they had fifty children each in their care and it would not have been possible for them to give every child the attention they needed. As Mr. Newbould said, "We did the best we could."

I asked Jessie about the clothing the children wore, considering it was wartime, and new clothes were difficult to obtain. She answered in her blunt manner, "Well, there were those children that didn't have a pair of knickers to their bottoms, if you know what I mean." I smiled because I did know what she meant.   Jessie continued, "Others were as well dressed as they could be. We had children from two orphanages, the Nutter Orphanage, which one of my ancestors founded, and these children always were well dressed. Teddy Tong was one of the Nutter children. I remember the gray suit and pullover he wore and it was all good quality."

The Cottage Home children were not so fortunate, Jessie said. "They wore navy blue suits that were made of a rough material. The difference between the clothing from the two orphanages was noticeable."

Teddy Tong said that he remembered always having chapped legs because of wearing short trousers. Jessie said, "In those days, a boy was fourteen before he went into long trousers. That was the way it was." She thought for a moment and said, "I suppose the boys must have been cold, but you didn't think about those things. Little boys just did wear short pants."

Mary recalled that some of the boys held their short pants up with rope and kept hitching them up with a hand at the back and one at the front.

The one boy that Jessie particularly remembered was Frances Cleghorn, who, she told me, "Always wore a heavy coat with large buttons. He wore it in the warm weather too," she said.

Ailsa said a boy called Arthur was given new clothes from the American Fund. His mother saw him in them and insisted he come home. Before he left, the boy went to Ailsa and told her that his mother would sell the new clothes if he went home in them. Ailsa said she felt "awful" but gave him the clothes he had worn when he arrived at the school. Arthur went home against his will and was so unhappy he ran away, going the thirty miles from Bradford to Linton on foot. Ailsa said when he returned he was filthy and covered in lice.

She said that it was sad that they had to send children back to homes like Arthur's. " I always felt sorry for the children who preferred the school to being at home. But at least these children knew there was a different way to live."

Ailsa said another boy had insisted the entire time he had been at Linton that he "hated the school." Mr. Sternwhite told him that, because he was fourteen, he would have to return home. Ailsa said the boy called Mr. Sternwhite "an old bugger" because he didn't want to leave.

Instead of a beating, he was given time to reflect. Finally, the young man was convinced that the decision for children to leave Linton at age fourteen was that of the Board of Education, not Mr. Sternwhite. The young man then said to Mr. Sternwhite, "You're as soft as toffee and I really would like to stay at school."

Tea was between five and six-thirty pm. Usually, we had tea or cocoa in the tin mugs, bread and butter, with runny jam and sometimes some tinned or dried fruit. It was seldom we had real fruit unless we got apples from the trees or wild blackberries or bilberries collected from bushes in the area. After tea, we went to school from six o'clock to seven-thirty.

Some former evacuees mentioned how the school had a good library and said it was there they had learned to appreciate books. Dorothy remembered that lights out was at 9:30 pm but said she read for a while with a torch under her blankets.

The popular children's books at the time were Enid Blyton, *Just William, Billy Bunter, Peter Pan, Wind in the Willows*, and a Linton favorite, Charles Kingsley's *The Water Babies*. Some of the children possibly read, Arthur Canon Doyle's, *Hound of the Baskervilles*, written about a hound living on the Devonshire Moors similar to the Barquest hound said to haunt the Cracoe Road close to Linton. For Christmas, the Beano and Dandy Annuals a compilation of the popular children's comics were a great favorite for those parents who could afford to buy them.

Maybe it was at Linton that I learned my love of reading. I also read with a torch, under the bedclothes. It was something I did for years.

Despite the interest in books for the few, it was not noticeable that the concentration was on the children's education. The age requirement at the school was for children from seven to fourteen. The skills taught at the school were vocational rather than educational. While Kennylands, a school also built by the Camps Corporation, had a science laboratory, Linton did not. If children passed the scholarship, like Dorothy and Teddy, they left Linton, and attended a Grammar School. This would be a difficult move for children who were orphans or had no family to take them in, or worse, did not want their children to continue their education.

Through a YMCA farming program, the Linton boys learned farming skills. When the men went into the services, young men were in demand to help run the farms.

The Women's Land Army filled in for many of the men from farms who went to war, and did a very good job. We would also see trucks full of Italian prisoners-of-war passing the school on their way to help on the farms. The Linton boys worked alongside the POW's, many of whom looked close to them in age.

Mary remembered that the older girls went out one afternoon a week by themselves before the arrival of the Italian POWs. After that she said, "Because of them our outings, ended. We were very upset."

Every week the Bradford Education Department brought parcels for the children to Linton. They had to wait to receive them until a teacher handed them out. Mary remembered the day, "There was a parcel with my name on it from my parents, so I opened it. I knew the rules and that I wasn't supposed to touch the parcel, but I did it anyway. The teachers found out and I was caned for disobeying orders."

All three women agreed, "We were all caned at some time."

In the first couple of years, the children had to stay at the school for the Christmas Holidays. Mary and Rose remembered spending their first Christmas at the school. They acted in a Christmas play that they also performed in the Grassington Town Hall. They went caroling around Linton village and to some of the outlying farms.

Rose and Mary received presents from their parents and decided to swap the gifts. Mary took the one from Roses' parents and she gave

Rose the one her parents brought for her. They said although they were not home with family for Christmas, "We made the best of it."

They decorated the dining hall with paper chains they had colored and hung. On Christmas day, they exchanged gifts. We did not get too much, but appreciated what we did receive a doll, book, game, or a knitted jumper. After Christmas lunch, we listened to the King's speech at 3 pm, played games and later had a dance. They said they had fun and even the young children stayed up late.

By the time I went to Linton most children went home for the holidays. I can clearly see the room next to the kitchen in Ravenscliffe on Christmas morning. It was freezing cold because mother had not had time to light the black leaded stove that took up one end of the room. When she lit the fire, she left Keith and me together while she went into the kitchen. She put on the kettle to make tea and I can still smell the bacon and eggs that she cooked on that cold morning. I hadn't seen a real egg for a long time. Whether we received gifts or not I cannot recall, but the smell of the food cooking and the gradual warmth of the room remain a cherished memory.

Rose stayed for five years at Linton, and became Head Girl before she left. Linton came under the jurisdiction of the Bradford council and during her time as Head Girl, the Lord Mayor of Bradford came to visit. Rose was one of the people introduced to him and she showed him around the school.

In the summer time, the Linton School had a sport's day to which the parent's were invited. The children took part in three-legged, wheelbarrow, egg and spoon races and generally enjoyed themselves. Unfortunately, because of the isolated location and parent's work schedules many parents were unable to attend.

Jessie said, "At Linton we were cocooned and isolated from much of what was happening in the world around us." While Linton may have appeared cut off from the regular world, Mary, Rose and Dorothy agreed that they certainly knew "there was a war on."

The sound of air-raid sirens regularly blasted the Linton children from sleep. The unmistakable sound meant that the children had to run to the cold and damp-smelling underground shelter with the cold metal bench. Sometimes Miss Fell or another teacher would read stories to calm the younger children as the planes continued to fly overhead.

The children so strongly objected to these regular disturbances and the uncomfortable shelter that the staff agreed to let them stay in their dormitories. There were however conditions. When the siren sounded, the children agreed to get under their beds. Mary said, "There wasn't much room underneath the bed for two children, but we preferred it to going into that awful, smelly shelter."

One night when the enemy planes were making their return trip over the moors, they heard a huge explosion, not far from the school. The next morning Winifred took the children to see what had happened. They walked through Grassington to Yarnbury where a land mine, jettisoned from one of the enemy planes, had landed. When she told me about this, Winifred said in her lovely Yorkshire brogue, "Oh love, the hole it made was so big you could have turned a bus around in it."

While some former evacuees give accounts of a plane going down in the area opposite the school, near the sanitarium, I have not been able to substantiate that as fact. Teddy Tong remembers being able to run over the hill to see the remains of a bomber that had crashed on the moor. The RAF guards, who would be young men little older than the Linton boys, evidently let them on to the site.

While I could not locate a plane that crashed in the Linton area, Jessie questioned people in Linton and they agreed that there was a downed plane in 1940 or 1941 flown by a Polish crew. It was a Lancaster bomber, whose pilot, disoriented by a severe snowstorm, crash-landed near the village of Cray. It would have been too far a distance for the children to walk to the crash-site, but not impossible. Some of the older boys may have been anxious enough to see the plane that they did indeed walk that far.

Several of the Linton boys, including Teddy Tong, went into the Royal Air Force. Their interest in planes may have come from their contact with downed aircraft and the different German airplanes they learned to recognize as they flew over the school.

Regardless, the children at the school had daily reminders that, "they lived in a country at war." The three former evacuees reflected on their wartime experiences, "Although we try to remember the happy times, it was a harsh, cold environment, we often were hungry, or bored with the food. We had to obey strict rules and what today we would consider slight infractions brought punishment with the cane. Worse, we were old enough to know the threat of invasion was always a possibility."

Mary stated firmly, "I have to say, Doreen, we made the most of our time at Linton but we had few possessions and there were no home comforts."

CHAPTER EIGHT

I n 2006, Frank Newbould died in Burley-in-Wharfedale, Yorkshire. Frank had attended the Church of England School in Burley and in 1957 became its headmaster. Until a month before his death, Frank sang in St Mary's Parish Church Choir, just as he had for 85 years after he joined as a boy. The villagers he had taught, grandparents to children, came to say farewell to the man they knew as "Mr. Burley."

On May 2, 2006, a Craven Herald & Pioneer reporter wrote about Frank Newbould and how he remembered gas lamps in the village and the "knocker-up" who went round the houses to wake the mill-workers. The reporter noted that Frank had taken rides on the first village trolley bus and on horse-drawn wagonettes. Frank was a historian who wrote for several publications on Burley-in-Wharfedale, St. Mary's Church and the Rotary Club, whose meetings he seldom missed. He was a lifelong member of the Otley Cricket Club, where he had been a player and past-president.

On 27 March 1997, Maundy Thursday, Frank was the recipient of Maundy money presented by Queen Elizabeth II at Bradford

Cathedral. This was only the fourth time in its 700-year history that Yorkshire hosted the ceremony.

Maundy money is awarded to British citizens eighty and over for their service to the community. Frank received the honor for his contribution to the education of children throughout his life. He proudly told my husband and me about meeting the Queen. "She handed me a red and a white pouch," he said. "The red pouch contained 71 coins, adjusted each year to the age of the Queen. They were special Maundy coins in the traditional values of 1, 2, 3, and 4 pence. The white pouch contained another 71 in current coins, two two-pound coins, a single one-pound coin and a fifty pence coin to the sum of five pounds and fifty pence." As a historian, Frank liked the tradition of the ceremony and proudly made a point of being factually accurate.

As a lifelong resident, Frank had become something of a landmark. When you saw him you knew exactly where you were. As the village vicar, the Rev. Michael Burley, said, "Frank had a passion for the church as well as the village. In the two years I've been here I don't think he ever missed a Sunday. He will leave a noticeable gap."

Mary Manley and Teddy Tong were two Linton evacuees who attended the funeral of Frank at the church he had attended since he was a boy. Frank Newbould had played an important part in the lives of all the Linton children.

Teddy spoke of the male role model Mr. Newbould had represented to him, teaching a love of sports that lasted a lifetime. My brother, Keith, who Frank said was an accomplished footballer, later played hockey for the British Army. He also credited Mr. Newbould with his ability to play and enjoy sports.

Frank was rightly proud of David Hackworth, a young man who had been a Linton evacuee. David went on to play football for Bradford City and for Sheffield United. Mr. Newbould followed this young man's career with great pride. I attempted to contact David or someone who might know how I could let him know what pleasure Mr. Newbould had taken in each of his successes. I would love to have brought the two together. My efforts were in vain.

The last time I visited Frank, I drove cautiously across the small bridge in Burley that led to his home in the shadow of St. Mary's church. Despite the fact that he was, as he said, "Legally blind," he greeted me warmly with a big smile and said, "It is good of you to come all the way from America to visit me." I miss his sharp mind and his exceptional memory and his letters written in copperplate handwriting. Frank Newbould left a gap in the lives of so many former pupils.

Frank vividly recalled arriving at Linton on 10 July 1940. "The Bradford Education Department gave us just three days notice that we had the job," he told me. "We just were thrown in at the deep-end." His memories were vivid, especially when it came to the organization of the school and the smell of the Canadian cedar, the wood used to construct the buildings.

I checked his memory. A local Bradford paper, *The Telegraph and Argus*, reported on 5 July 1940, "Each school cost £20,000 and the huts, built of British Columbia cedar wood, were lined with asbestos compound."

Mr. Newbould at age 89 could still rattle off the dormitory names that reflected the Yorkshire dales: Garthfield, Piper Bank, Cringles, Kirkholme, Longdales. He also remembered every teacher's name: Miss Ormanroyd, Mrs. Woodhead, Miss Miles, Mr. Essem, Miss Mayo,

Miss Pickering, Miss Dickinson, Mrs. Ellison, Miss Hammond, and Miss Hindle (Lowcock).

He rummaged through his memories for me, pulling out one unrelated detail after another as I furiously wrote. There was "no running water in the dormitory building," he said, "and they were very 'austere.' They weren't really built for comfort." The whole site was 35 acres and he was pleased with the Linton playing fields: "You could have put two football pitches and two cricket pitches on them. The amount of space was wonderful."

He repeatedly told me that, "no thought of, or at any rate provision, had been made to deal with clothing repairs. At first, there were no supplies and most of the children had brought only a minimum of clothing."

Frank continued, "Because it was July, when the school opened Mr. Sternwhite decided we should be on holiday." He laughed. "Although it sounded good, it was hard work arranging 'activities' for the children all day until they went to bed at night. I kept the boys out on the soccer and cricket fields and we had them practicing until we tired them out. We went inside on bad days, put on the radiogram and taught them to dance. We were all grateful for that radiogram and the records. It was a case of when in doubt, dance."

"In the early days," he said, "we worked for two months without a break. Then they began to bring in 'floaters' who relieved us, so we could take time off. Working all those hours and exercising so much with the boys, I was often exhausted when I finally went to sleep."

One night the air-raid siren went off and the older boys hurried to the air-raid shelter. After a while someone asked, "Where's Mr. Newbould?"

When the all-clear sounded and the boys returned to their dormitory, Frank was still in his bed, sound asleep. "I was so tired that night that I slept right through the air-raid and didn't hear a thing." He said, "The boys and the staff never let me forget it."

Mr. Newbould had worked with Mr. Sternwhite on what he called the first evacuation of Bradford children in 1939. Throughout the country, a large number of children had been evacuated. Historians call this the "phony war"—Poland had been invaded and war had been declared. It just wasn't yet being fought. When the predicted bombing did not materialize, the children began to return home.

Mr. William Sternwhite volunteered to head the Linton Residential School. Mr. Sternwhite was in charge of everything involved with the children's education and their welfare. All the teachers and the nurse were his responsibility. The task was daunting in that, unlike many of the Camp Schools, he did not take over an entire school that moved in as a group.

"The Linton children came from forty different schools," Frank Newbould explained. "The Bradford Education Department closed orphanages and sent those children to Linton. Although many of the teachers knew one another, Mr. Sternwhite was dealing with several he had not worked with previously. None of them had worked in a boarding school situation." Frank said, "We learned the job by trial and error."

When the first Bradford evacuees became homesick and went home, Ailsa told me the children who replaced them were "some of the most difficult of Bradford's children."

Winifred agreed. "We got the children no one else would take," she said.

All the teachers attributed Mr. Sternwhite's management of the school for their being able to manage such a variety of children, who ran the gamut from the very smart to those who had severe social and learning disabilities. The school did not have any social workers, but, as Winifred said, "We had to fill that role as well as teach."

Mr. Sternwhite's model called for each dormitory to have a family-like atmosphere with the housemistress or housemaster acting as substitute parents. There is a picture of Mr. Sternwhite, complete with pipe, with Mrs. Ellison sitting outside a dormitory having tea with a small group of girls. He tried to get the teachers to take on the role of parent, something difficult to do with so many children. He thought these children, who had been taken from everything familiar, needed one person in their lives to give them stability.

He requested that the teachers "keep the children busy with lessons, games, walks, swimming in the Wharfe, sports and dancing. We have to occupy their time." His ideas for the school were different from any tried before.

The Bradford authority certainly tested his and the Linton staff's abilities with the different levels of children they sent to the school. For this reason, his biggest supporters were the teachers who, although tested by the difficult children, tried to help him accomplish those goals. Although the workday was long and challenging, they agreed that Mr. Sternwhite gave them guidance and supported them. They always knew they could depend on him.

Maintaining the school site and buildings and the kitchen and ground staff was the responsibility of Mr. C. A. Davidson.

All the teachers agreed that Sternwhite and Davidson did not get along. According to Winifred, "Mr. Davidson was the only thorn in our side. " On July 5, 1940, prior to the children arriving at Linton, Mr. Davidson told the *Telegraph* and *Argus*, "I think camp life will do the boys and girls so much good that their mothers will not know them after they have been here for a short time." Mr. Sternwhite and Mr. Davidson lived in bungalows next to one another and had the only cars on the school site. Their negative attitudes toward each other must have affected the day-to-day running of the school.

When Winifred first went to Linton she said she was a little "taken aback" by the small, spartan room she was assigned on the "Little Girl's Dormitory."

"The staff bedroom had a single iron bedstead, a chair and a chest we named 'The Coffin,' for one's belongings," she said. "Needless to say, we gradually refurnished our own rooms to make them more comfortable. On my first weekend off, I went to Brown Muffs and bought a divan bed, a Lloyd loom chair, and a bureau with four large drawers. We put the coffin outside the door and stood it up. The handyman put a bar across and I used it as a wardrobe."

Winifred explained that the staff's washing facilities were directly behind those for the children. "So we had to troop across in all weather to wash and shower the children and ourselves."

Alongside the interview with Mr Davidson, the *Telegraph* and *Argus* gave this description of the Linton dining facility: "The dining room is so roomy that all the children can be fed at one sitting. In the adjoining kitchen there are huge ovens and bottlers, and the latest devices for dealing with food in bulk, including a machine for cutting and buttering bread at the rate of 60 slices per minute." None of the staff mentioned the bread cutting and buttering machine, but it had to be innovative at the time.

Winifred explained, "At one end of the dining hall was the headmaster's study and at the other, the staff room. This was a very pleasant room with windows on three sides. Here we had our meals when not on duty and relaxed in the bit of spare time we had. The room became more comfortable when Mrs. Ellison, who had given up her home in Bradford, brought with her a three-piece suite and a piano. We all appreciated the gesture."

Fate had given Mr. Sternwhite an ironic name, according to Winifred's recollections. "Mr. Sternwhite insisted that the children on our dormitory were our responsibility and we had to take care of them. He would say something to us if the children did not look clean or have tidy hair. In the first two years, we even darned socks for the children. During the afternoons, I became expert at taking parties of children to Grass Woods, down to the Linton Church stepping-stones and to the Hebden swing-bridge. Mr. Sternwhite's advice was, "Always lead from the back, never go on in front."

"One year, Kilney Agricultural Show was being held, so two staff took a party of children there walking the three to four miles each way. I was in the dormitory when the children came back. They staggered in and flopped down on their beds. One little Irish girl, Millie Mullaney, summed it up, 'Eh Miss, it were a toil of a pleasure!'

"We often didn't come off duty until 9:30 or 10:00 pm after putting the children to bed and reading them a story," Winifred continued. "I always waited until they went to sleep. Then in the summer, we went for bike rides, because with the double summer time it was light until midnight.

"We also had some lovely sociable evenings in the Staff Room, singing to the accompaniment of Ellie's piano or playing Mahjong or other games. We gradually gelled into one really happy family and the children meant a lot to us. I can honestly say we were dedicated to them."

Games were one thing, but unexpected adventures formed the basis for lasting memories. "One weekend there was a heavy snowfall on the Friday evening after two of us had arrived in Bradford for a weekend off," Winifred said. "We heard that the buses weren't running but the trains were, so we decided to get a train to Skipton. We then planned to walk the rest of the way, approximately a ten mile hike."

Winifred's father had been Chief Air Raid Precautions Warden for the area for years. After the Skipton experience, she recalled, he "took us to the Depot and kitted us out with waterproofs and Wellingtons and we duly set off. When the train arrived in Skipton it was still snowing. The snow had filled up the roads so most of the way we kept to the field's. It was a cold, tiring walk, but we were young and did not give it much thought at the time. We staggered into the Devonshire Arms at Cracoe at about 6 o'clock in the evening. After having a hot drink a farmer took us the rest of the way in his truck. When we walked into Linton, we were the 'heroines' of the hour. The staff did not expect to see us for several days. However, we were back on duty again at 7:30 am the next morning.

"While we could have made the excuse that the buses weren't running and stayed at home. We did not think twice about it. We felt a loyalty to the other teachers and knew they would do the same for us."

In 2006, one of the boys told me that the school's electrician, Charles Lowcock, began coming to the school after work hours to visit Winifred. "We used to follow and spy on them when they were courting," he said. "I do not know if Winifred was aware of this, but it must have seemed like having two hundred bothersome brothers and sisters."

Winifred said, "We had some teachers who were strict with the children, but Miss Ormanroyd was not. Mr. Sternwhite took her on anyway. One day one of the children in her class threw himself on the floor and began to scream. Despite the pleas of Miss Ormanroyd Jimmy would not stop. Miss Fell, a small, older teacher who took care of the little boys walked in and said, 'Jimmy, you get up off the floor this minute and stop making that silly noise.'" To everyone's amazement, Jimmy did, and never behaved that way again.

Frank said that everyone spoke of the efficiency of Nurse O'Connor, who was well-liked and very particular about the running of the clinic. "Thanks to her," Frank said, "We did not have an epidemic of any kind during my time at Linton. She made sure the children showered one day and strip washed the next. They were the cleanest children around. We did have a boy with diphtheria, but the nurse put him into quarantine and then sent him to a Bradford hospital. The rest of the school did not get it."

At that time, children's diseases spread quickly through the schools. Children died from diseases that are curable today. I asked Mary if she used the same spoon for the children when we had the malt and cod-liver oil each day. Mary said, "No, Nurse O'Connor was fussy about using a different spoon for each child. I had to put them in a special container after we used them."

Winifred smiled. "Nurse O'Connor's biggest problem was head lice. Some of the children came with them. Nurse O'Connor would work hard to get rid of them and then families would make their monthly visit. As soon as they left, the nurse would start again making sure that the children's heads were clear. When she was sure that all the children were clear, the monthly visit would occur and she would have to begin again."

She also told me, "Nurse O'Connor had a suitor who was a Bradford Police Inspector. The problem was, she was a Catholic and he was not. In those days, you did not marry outside your Catholic religion." Winifred told me Nurse O'Connor often said, "'My parents would have a fit if I married someone outside the church.' Nurse O'Connor went back to Killarney and married a Catholic. I went to visit her there on several occasions. She was a really good person and a good friend."

Ailsa had some different stories to tell about the children. In her job as Welfare Officer, she saw them in another light.

"On my first morning at Linton I was sent all the enuretics to deal with," Aisla told me, "I did not know what an enuretic was. I soon learned though – there were a number of bed-wetters. The first was a lanky boy of about thirteen with lots of violet blue blotches on his face. I thought some one had been throwing ink at him. No, he was a bedwetter and the blotches were gentian-violet ointment. I had to issue him with a new sleeping bag as with all the others who followed him."

Ailsa said, "I found myself increasingly concerned with the less fortunate children at the school, of which there were many. Several of the original evacuees had returned home and they sent troublesome children from downtown Bradford. I had to go every so often by bus to collect them after they had medicals at the Bradford School Clinic. I had to check that they had two of every item of clothing and then bring them back to Linton by bus. I found the 30 mile journey too much in one day so I would go and stay the night and bring them back the next day."

"Some children arrived at Linton without adequate clothing. We had an arrangement with a group of kindhearted Americans who became 'Foster parents' to some of the more deprived children. Frank described the large wooden crates of used, but very good clothing and shoes that regularly arrived from The American Fund."

Ailsa was concerned about the parents who sent their children to the school without suitable clothing. She said, "I remember one little girl came in the middle of winter with only a cotton dress and a pair of thin knickers. I soon dressed her in lovely warm clothes from my store of garments I had amassed from the American Fund. I very quickly realized that some of these Bradford parents were deliberately sending children inadequately clothed. Soon after they arrived they would want the child returned home. If they went home in their new clothes, the parents sold them. We believe that the first children who came to Linton were provided with new clothes, so the word spread when so many of them went home."

"This little girl was a case in point, but by this time I was wise and I always put the garments they came in away and when they went home sent them back as they had come. I always felt terrible doing so. I could tell you a lot more stories like this, but it would become boring."

Ailsa recalled that, "While I was at Linton there were many disturbed and disruptive children, but I never remember any brutal punishment being meted out. Mr. Sternwhite certainly knew how to handle difficult children, and many of them improved tremendously while at the school."

"I particularly remember one girl called Nora. She went to Linton via the Child Guidance Clinic where they called her, 'The worst girl in Bradford.' I can remember thinking at the time, how could anyone have said such a thing. Had they met every girl in Bradford? She certainly was very disturbed. She had a very bad home life, with a mother who had many men around her. She went home one time to help her mother have a child. The tales she told when she came back do not bear repeating."

Nora settled down to Mr. Sternwhite's way of discipline and two years later the children voted her Head Girl, with the approval of the staff. Ailsa said, "I used to see her years later in Bradford and she earned her living as a bus conductress. She made quite a good home for herself and her son. Nora told Ailsa, 'Although I made the same mistake as my mother, I shall always make sure my son is well looked after.'"

Even though the teachers were dealing with many children with learning or social disabilities, they did not receive extra pay for their long hours.

One Christmas, Ailsa took some of the boys to the Bradford pantomime. When they got off the bus in Bradford one of the boys said, "Missus, I could run home from here, I live just up the road." Ailsa told him, "That's all right, love, why don't you go home and we'll go to the pantomime?" Ailsa said she knew the little boy would rather be at Linton than living with his family.

Ailsa told a lovely story about one Christmas when many of the children had gone home and only the orphans who had nowhere to go remained. The children did not have anyone to buy Christmas gifts for them. Mr. Sternwhite, the headmaster, gave her some money to buy gifts for them. On Christmas Eve, she told the boys to hang up their stockings for Father Christmas. She said the children looked at her in amazement and exclaimed, "E'll never leave us nutthin missus, 'e never'as." Ailsa said to them, "You lived in the city and Father Christmas probably could not find you there. Why don't you hang your stockings, just to see?" she told them.

Ailsa explained to me that she did not drink, but that evening went to the Linton pub to a dance and she did have one drink. That night after returning to the dormitory, she carefully filled each stocking with "an orange, a few sweets and some small toys."

Very early the next morning she awakened to the sound of the children's voice as they clustered under the Sani-Lav light to open their stockings. Miss Williams said, "I will never forget the look on those little boy's faces when they realized the stockings were full." The children beamed as they told her, "You were right missus, 'e did find us."

Ailsa laughed. "Those little boys who had been labeled as difficult were as good as gold, at least for the rest of the holiday." She remarked,

"It was such moments that made life in that harsh environment worthwhile."

Jessie said, "I was afraid of everything, including the children when I went to the school. I was only twenty-two and had not done much teaching before. They called me a floater, because I relieved the regular teachers so they could take time off."

According to Jessie, by the time she arrived at Linton, women from the village had come to live in small rooms in the housekeeping block and spent their time washing, sewing and mending the children's clothing. One of the local women, Sheila, went with Jessie to Grassington on the weekend to the local dance, which included country dancing.

"We were certainly isolated at Linton. When the children went to bed at nights we would go for bike rides in the summer, and in the winter we went to Grassington on the weekend to the dance at the Town Hall. We would sometimes get a taxi and go. There were never many men at the dance because of the war, so we danced with other women."

Every Tuesday night there was choir practice at Linton. The entire school could participate and Jessie, because of her musical background, was "encouraged" to lead the choir. "I didn't like conducting," Jessie said, so eventually, "I ended up playing the piano. We had fun with those evenings and I know the children must have learned all the songs we sang, everything from *Fight the Good Fight*, to *Jeannie with the Light Brown Hair*, and Mary Manley's favorite, *Here in the Country's Heart*. All our songs came from the National Song Book, which I do not think they use today, or so Jessie told me. The children learned the music even if they never joined the choir. Jessie smiled, "We may not have sounded good, but we certainly made a lot of noise."

Ella Pontefact, in her book *Wharfedale*, speaks about the local fairs in our part of England. "The climax of the feast was the dance which followed it. The local fiddler,… would play, and old country dances,… some of which originated in this district, would be danced. The dalespeople have loved dancing as they loved music; in 1783 there was a dancing master in Buckden."

Finding themselves as isolated as some of those dales villages, it is hardly surprising that the Linton School maintained many of the local customs when its staff were from the surrounding areas.

Jessie said the school had a set of Shinty Sticks, a Scottish game resembling hockey played with a wooden ball. Jane, an exceptionally quiet older girl, decided that she would love to roll the wooden "Shinty Ball" down the dormitory when everyone was asleep—just to see what would happen. She did not tell anyone about it, but one evening at midnight when everyone was asleep, she rolled the ball down the dormitory and hopped back into bed. According to Jessie, "The ball was wooden and made a dickens of a noise. She woke the entire dormitory, including Miss Hammond."

Miss Hammond, of course, demanded to know who the culprit was. Evidently, when Jane told her, "It was me," Miss Hammond said, "You wouldn't do something like that. It could not have been you. You're covering for someone else." The more the girl insisted that it was her, the less Miss Hammond believed her.

Each child earned Red Dots for good behavior. If they did something negative, they lost the Red Dots and their privileges. As a result, the entire dormitory of girls lost their "Red Dots" that week. No one went out that weekend from Miss Hammond's dorm despite Jane's persistent confessions.

One of the things I learned from Jessie in 2008 was that all the staff caned the children. None of the others had mentioned it to me. "Oh yes we did; we had to, and I hated it," said Jessie.

While the staff taught the children math, geography, history, English and the various sports, there were two individuals from Linton village who came to the school to teach extra-curricular subjects to the children. Dr. Arthur Raistrick was one of them, an archeologist, geologist and WWII conscientious objector, who lived in Linton.

Dr. Raistrick was an intense, tweed-wearing, taciturn man, who frequently came to the school to speak to the children. As the locals said, "What Dr. Raistrick didn't know about the Dales wasn't worth knowing." He had written books about the history and methods of building those thousand of miles of stonewalls that zigzagged the moors. He was an authority on lead mining, a thriving industry on the Yorkshire Moors from Roman Times until the late 1800s. Mining, both silver and lead, had once employed large numbers of people, including my great-grandfather as a lead miner, and my great-grandmother's father, a mining engineer.

He made the children aware of how dangerous the disused mines could be if they played near them. Jessie remembered the children telling her to watch out for the mines that were "everywhere on the moors." The children would say, "We know because Dr. Raistrick told us."

Dr. Raistrick wrote about the shepherds who tended the thousands of sheep whose wool was gathered and woven in the industrial towns nearby. He spoke of the German (Jaeger) origins of the wild ponies used as pack animals to carry the wool, lead or silver ore. He told the children those pack-ponies were the ancestors of the wild ponies that still roamed the moors.

Dr. Raistrick told the children that there were over 200 Iron- and Bronze-age sites in the area. He would show them Calf Hole where traces of men from the Iron Age, were found. Further along the road is the Druids' Circle a Mid-Bronze Age circle of four standing stones. He would describe how they should be careful when they played around these sites. The dales were a busy thriving lead mining community centuries before the arrival of the Angles, the Romans and the Danes. It was from the Norsemen that dalesfolk got their blunt stubbornness and many of the words in their language: Blubberhouses, Yockenthwaite, bairn, laikin – words Scandinavians today recognize in the Yorkshire dialect.

One of the trips on which Dr. Raistrick probably took the children was across the pretty, if unusual, Emily's bridge, a local landmark named for Emily Norton. He would tell the children how she, as a young girl, fled from soldiers in the civil war and found sanctuary with the miller who lived over the bridge renamed in her memory. Generations of brides and mourners crossed Emily's bridge on their way to Linton Church on their wedding days or when carried to their funerals. My husband loved the Dales' gray stone bridges and painted many of them, including a view of Emily's Bridge that hangs in my living room today.

Jessie Robson remembered how the boys would take her to places she considered out of bounds for them. Jessie said, "I would tell them, we can't go in there." But the children would say to her, "Oh, no Miss, Dr. Raistrick took us in there to see the leat. It's a trench that brings water to the mill. We can go in Miss." They would lead Jessie to the site and pass on verbatim the information the good doctor had told them. Jessie said, "The children remembered everything he said."

Mary remembered going to Dr. Raistrick's home, a converted barn in Linton. She said, "There was a beautiful new carpet on the stairs and when I walked up them I took off my shoes. I was embarrassed because I had holes in my stockings." She is not sure whether Dr. Raistrick told her to remove her shoes, or whether because she did not want to get dirt on such a lovely carpet.

While many adults thought Dr. Raistrick "difficult to deal with," the Linton children "loved him and absorbed everything he told them." Dr. Raistrick was a respected University lecturer, a fact that would be unknown to the children. He was a legend on the moors and had an amazing knowledge that the children were fortunate to share.

In later life, Dr. Raistrick looked like a slight Albert Schweitzer, with his halo of white hair. When I inquired in Grassington about talking with him, several of the local people told me, "He is such an old curmudgeon." Dr. Raistrick died in April 1991. He supported the Linton School from its inception and gave a great deal of his time to the evacuees. I believe if I had told Dr. Raistrick that I had been a Linton evacuee he may have taken the time to talk with me. Unfortunately, I will never know.

Mrs. Halliwell Sutcliffe, wife of the romantic novelist, was another celebrated guest at Linton. Her husband wrote *The Striding Dales*, a collection of stories, some of which had roots that stretched back centuries. His widow came to the school and also made the children welcome at her home. Unfortunately, the children thought Mrs. Sutcliffe "looked like a witch," so they did not want to spend time with her. They do not remember Mrs. Sutcliffe telling her husband's stories, but I like to think she did. He wrote such rich and colorful prose, full of admiration for his surroundings.

Halliwell Sutcliffe wrote the story of Sir William Craven, the Dales' own Dick Whittington, who, without the cat, went from his lowly beginnings in Appletreewick to seek his fortune in London. He found work with a London merchant, worked hard and was fortunate to marry his master's daughter. William Craven became Lord Mayor of London while still in his teens. He returned to Appletreewick as Sir William Craven where he built Burnsall Bridge and Burnsall School, one of the most beautiful buildings in the dales. Locals said he was a man whose riches brought no arrogance.

Sutcliffe also wrote about the Yorkshire highwayman, Nevison, known as "Riding Will", who is reputed to have sheltered at Percival Hall, not far from Linton. Law enforcement searched in vain for him. Riding Will was the northern Robin Hood who protected the innocent, taking from the rich and giving to the poor. The law caught up with Riding Will and he ended up in York jail. With the help of a doctor friend Will convinced the governor of the jail he had the plague. The governor was afraid of the illness and refused to visit him. With the doctor's assistance Will, "died" and was "buried outside the jail." He escaped the coffin as soon as it left York jail and continued his life as Riding Will.

Herbert Sutcliffe died in 1932, eight years before the school opened. I like to think it would have been him and not his wife who relayed these stories to the children with the wonderful flourishes with which he wrote.

At the Reunion in 2006, many evacuees thanked their former teachers for being "surrogate parents" during their time away from their families. Most of these pupils had not known that these teachers were still alive. To some, it was only in retrospect that they realized the value of their time at the school. With hindsight, they could recognize the sincerity of the teachers and their genuine commitment to their young charges.

The women remembered identifying with female teachers, who they said, "really cared." A phrase that frequently ran through the conversations was, "We were a family." One man remembered the older children taking care of "the little 'uns."

Two male former evacuees said, "There were lumps in our throats when we saw the ugly remains of the Linton school. We spent some of the happiest days of our lives there and hate to see it this way."

Dr. Sternwhite would have been pleased to hear that at least some of the children said, "We were family." That was his goal.

Despite the fact that many of the children were orphans, had lost one parent, had social or educational difficulties, Frank believed the staff's dedication overcame those odds. Frank said, "We tried to make Linton a safe haven for children from the turmoil and craziness of war."

While the children may or may not have attained a certain level of academic achievement, they did learn to appreciate the beauty of their surroundings. They learned the culture of the dales and the legacy left by the people who had lived centuries ago as well as the more recent lead miners, shepherds, and farmers. Everyone learned a sport, to sing, and they all learned to dance.

Winifred said, "I do not see the desolation when I pass by the locked gate of Linton School, I don't see ruined buildings. I hear the happy sound of children playing and the school bell ringing."

CHAPTER NINE

One of the most important incidents that happened during my search for my lost childhood was in 1980. My Uncle Howard, mother's youngest brother, died in May of that year. Hazel, his wife, found the wallet he had carried with him when he served abroad for five years during the war. The wallet contained the following letter written by my mother. In it mother explained her story as clearly as if she had recorded it on tape.

Jessie Elizabeth Drewry, 10 Damon Avenue,

Ravenscliffe, Bradford, Yorks, 7 September 1943,

S/480945 H.C. Lowe,Sgt. FASC. 10 Stationery Dept,

Middle East Force.

Dear Howard,

I have just been along to mothers and your parcel of   fruit   looks very good. I get more disgusted every time I go home. I have nothing to thank any of them for.

I am feeling very lonely. Doreen and Keith are both away so that I can work, but I shall be glad when I can have them home. If Alan had lived, he would have been 14 yesterday.

I am working on Idle and Thackley district at present. It is very hilly though. The other nurse has a car but I am not able to drive so have to walk.

Doreen says tell Uncle Howard I want a monkey when he comes back. Perhaps you would send them a card from where you are. Their address is:

> Doreen and Keith Drewry
> Linton Residential School
> Linton, Nr. Skipton, Yorks.

I have not seen Vincent for a good long time. Annie, Syd and Brian have been home this last week they look very well. I was at Cousin Alices' last week. You know Stanley Douglas is playing for Undercliffe and he got his 1,000th wicket. He got a mounted ball and a present from the club. He is the first Bradford man to get it, he will be captain next year.

Hurry up and come back home. We shall all be glad to see this lot is over won't we?

I am going to see Doreen and Keith on Sunday but it hurts me when none of the family, think of buying them anything, not even a few biscuits. But they can buy for other children. I won't forget.

> Well, Howard do write to me won't you.
> Best of Health, Luck and Happiness from your sister, Jessie

How I wish I had been able to see the letter before my mother's death. While she seemed unwilling or unable to explain her situation to me this letter was a treasure trove of information, for which I shall always be grateful. I could hear in every sentence my mother explaining to me the difficulties of wartime life, why she had to send my brother and me away, and, why she remarried. This is my interpretation of the letter:

Dear Howard,

I have just been along to mothers and your parcel of fruit looks very good. I get more disgusted every time I go home. I have nothing to thank any of them for.

The comment about the fruit that Howard sent to his parents emphasizes how rare and difficult it was to obtain such delicacies during the war. Mother remarks on how good the fruit looked -- which clearly indicates that she did not sample any. Her bitter comments that she is "disgusted with them" and "has nothing to thank them for" further validates the point that she was not offered any part of Howard's parcel.

Besides the apples we saw in the summer growing on the local trees, oranges are the only other fruit I can remember seeing during the war. Women queued to get them because it was so seldom they were available. Wartime fruit came mostly dried or out of a tin. I thought for years that mandarin oranges and pears only came in tins. We only read about bananas, but did not see any until 1945-46 when the war with Germany was over. Most people who lived through the wartime food shortages can remember the first time they saw or tasted a banana.

The memories of bananas were so strong that Myra Schneider wrote a poem about her first memories of seeing one.

Drawing a Banana,
A Memory of Childhood during Wartime.

Forty of us looked longingly at the yellow finger
Plumped, curved, bearing strange black marks.

The word "banana" purred insistently around the classroom.
Our teacher, furrowed by severity as much as age,
Smiled slight, then mounted her trophy on a box for us
To draw with thick pencil on thin, grey page.

It was boring drawing that banana. My leaden lines
Smudged with rubbings out didn't resemble the fruit taunting
My hungry eyes. I couldn't quite remember seeing
A "live" banana before – there was a war to fight
And grown-ups said we had to go without and make do.
Yet if I closed my eyes I could conjure up a feast of sight:

 A window of violet-iced cakes and chocolates heaped
On silver trays belonging to a piece of magic time
As far as my certainty stretched back war enveloped all
War meant somber ships sliding slowly down the Clyde,

Sirens,snuggling with cocoa in the cupboard beneath the stairs
Though the only bomb that fell was on the moors and no one died.

Seeing a banana for the first time was a memory no one forgot.
One evening mother gave me a banana, and I remember how excited
I was and how good it tasted. Later, I attended a brownie meeting and
had to leave early with terrible stomach pains, I imagine it was because
we were not used to eating fresh fruit, particularly bananas.

*I am feeling very lonely. Doreen and Keith are both away
so that I can work, but I shall be glad when I can have them
home. If Alan had lived, he would have been 14 yesterday.*

Mother wrote this letter on 7 September 1943, less than a year after my father had died. She mentions her eldest son, Alan, and his death. Four losses in a matter of a few short years would be difficult for any mother to bear.

Too frequently children died of what we would consider minor illnesses. In the 1930s and 1940s, the medical profession was not as enlightened nor did they have the technological advances that we have today.

The sentence was, *"Doreen and Keith are both away so I can work."* Her ten-shilling-a-week government widow's pension would not keep one person, let alone three. She could not both work to keep a roof over our heads and put food on the table. She did not have the luxury of social programs that would take care of her needs. She had to take care of them herself.

*I am working on Idle and Thackley district at present. It is
very hilly though. The other nurse has a car but I am not able
to drive so have to walk.*

Mother had worked on night duty as a nurse at the General Electric Munitions factory. She often spoke of the dances they had during the night at the factory and how they would smoke when they had breaks. Smoking was common amongst British woman and a habit many, including mother, took up during the war. It must have been a relief from stress. No one told them it was dangerous for their health.

Mother probably changed her job in order to work during the day. Unfortunately, "the Idle and Thackley district" that she references is a large and hilly area. Having to use public transport and to walk to visit each patient had to be exhausting. There were few cars on the roads and few petrol coupons to run a car if you did have one. Because she did not know the area, mother had to rely on local people to direct her to the different patient's homes.

It was while mother was working as a district nurse that she met my stepfather, Cecil Oldfield. He had a sweets and tobacconists shop in Idle. We never understood why she married him. He was a sicker man than my father. Mother had to nurse him for the rest of his life. It was only after reading this letter after her death, and her comment *"...I shall be glad when I can have them home,"* that I realized. She married him to get us out of the Linton school. Unfortunately, Keith never did come home to live.

I have not seen Vincent for a good long time. Annie, Syd and Brian have been home this last week, they look very well.

This paragraph suggests how she longed to "get back to the way thing were." These are the mundane comments about family that one might speak about in peacetime. She comments on not seeing her eldest brother Vincent, who did not serve in the war. Her sister Annie's husband served in a medical unit in Devon. He was able to have his wife and son with him. This was mother's attempt to put the clock back and talk about normal family happenings.

I was at Cousin Alice's last week. You know Stanley Douglas is playing for Undercliffe and he got his 1,000th wicket. He got a mounted ball and a present from the club. He is the first Bradford man to get it, he will be captain next year.

There is nothing more "normal" for anyone born in Yorkshire than cricket. For many years, only someone born in Yorkshire could play cricket for the county. Yorkshire people loved the sport and the cricketers. My Uncle Howard played cricket and so did my mother. Stanley Douglas, her cousin Alice's husband's, success at the game would be of interest to Howard. They would also remind him of the cricket pitch on a sunny day in England and the normalcy of life, even in wartime. After almost three years in the Egyptian desert, he must have longed to enjoy simple pleasures.

Doreen says tell Uncle Howard I want a monkey when he comes back. Perhaps you would send them a card from where you are.

We thought the place Howard had gone was so foreign. And it was. He was in Egypt, but we would not have known that at the time. The censors were very strict about checking to see that we did not know the whereabouts of military personnel. Mother did know he was in the Middle East. I must have associated any place that was hot – and somehow we knew that – with monkeys and thought I could have one as a pet.

Hurry up and come back home. We shall all be glad to see this lot over won't we?

Having been like a mother to Howard, she wanted him to "Hurry up and come back home," longing to see him out of harm's way. Service members left the country and thousands did not see their families for five or six years.

"We will be glad to see this lot's over," in reference to the war was a common wartime expression. After four years of war, the British had

had enough of shortages. They were tired of civilian and military casualties, bombings, air raid sirens, nights' in shelters, and separation from loved ones. Additionally, they longed to live with more than the bare necessities of life: shops without shortages, and living with the constant fear of invasion. After three years in desert conditions Howard, and every other Briton, would have heartily agreed with her.

I am going to see Doreen and Keith on Sunday but it hurts me when none of the family, think of buying them anything, not even a few biscuits. But they can buy for other children. I won't forget.

The Bradford Education Department decided that it would be disruptive for children to see their parents more often than once a month. Mother came each month to visit us at the school. Her sister, Annie, came with her on one occasion, but I cannot remember anyone else coming to see us at Linton.

I remember the occasion distinctly because we all walked into Grassington and had lunch at the Devonshire Arms. The waiter hovered over the table and whisked away plates if he thought you were finished. My aunt ordered Brown Windsor Soup, which many will remember because during the war restaurants made it from a powder. The powder would get lumpy, stick to your teeth and taste awful. My aunt put her soupspoon down for a second, and the remains of her lumpy Brown Windsor soup disappeared from the table in a flash. None of us can remember the rest of the meal, but for years, we laughed about the waiter who prematurely took Aunt Annie's soup.

It had to be disturbing for mother not to have the support of her family at such a time. Grandmother made toys for the children of her doctor and the minister. While she could have paid "in kind" for the doctor, I do not think it likely that she owed the same to the minister. It was confusing also to know that these children were far more privileged than were we.

Mother did not forget. We moved to the South of England after the war. Although she and her husband bought her parent's house, she did not visit often. We went for Christmas our first year away and later mother went to see her father of whom she was very fond.

> *Well, Howard do write to me won't you.*
> *Best of Health,*
> *Luck and Happiness from your sister, Jessie*

At this time, writing to her brother must have seemed a way out of a crushing loneliness. She worked, but the people she nursed were ill and confined to their homes. Each evening she returned to the emptiness of her home, no husband, no children, and a brother overseas "for the duration," the ultimate reminders of her loneliness. The health, the luck and the happiness had to be attributes she wished for herself as well as for her brother. The letter shouts out for an end to "this lot", as many called the war, a yearning to give up the shortages and worries associated with a country at war and a return to a normal life.

I consider myself extremely fortunate to have been given this letter. I would like to have spoken to my mother about the war and her feelings about having to send us away. Reliving that time for her would have been an extremely difficult task. My father's death together with the long-standing tradition of "not speaking about family matters" made the task, for her, impossible. She simply could not bring herself to talk about that time of her life.

The words she wrote helped me to understand how she felt and what her options were. I do not believe there was an alternative for her but to send us away.

The letter is Mother's account of her life during the war spelled out for me in her own words. I doubt that today's mothers would be willing to change their lives for hers or those of any other parent who "sent their children away." When people live in a wartime situation, everything changes. It was not an easy way to live.

Mother's letter to Howard gave me an answer to the question so many evacuees want answered: "Why did you send me away?"

During the search for my lost childhood, I set out to find out why my mother sent us away. Her letter suggests that she had no option. The government required her services for the war effort, when she needed to be with my father. Her work as a nurse served both purposes. After his death, she had to work to feed herself and her children. In that letter, I found the answer to my question.

The other question that had troubled me for years was, why had she married my stepfather? He was a sick man when she married him and she looked after him until he died in 1958. Her marriage did not give her much pleasure or let her take life easy.

Mother met my stepfather when he was her patient while she was covering Idle as a district nurse.

Cecil Oldfield, was much older than mother. At age eighteen, photos show him in his Scots Guard uniform, his red and white banded hat set at a jaunty angle. Shortly after his nineteenth birthday, gassed and injured, he was left for dead on a World War I battlefield in France.

Mustard gas caused a weak heart, and the shrapnel in his head, violent headaches. He had three paralyzed fingers on his right hand.

Prior to the war, Cecil had played the violin and been captain of his cricket team. On his return from France, he could do neither. My stepfather dealt with his misfortune by shutting himself off from the world, like a tortoise, seldom sticking his head out, or allowing anyone to penetrate his ever-thickening shell.

Because of my stepfather's heart problems, the doctor recommended a move from the harsh northern winters of Yorkshire to milder southern climes. We moved to Devonshire after the winter of 1947, which was particularly severe. When we moved my brother, Keith did not move with us. Mother's dream of having the family re-united never materialized.

My stepfather could go for days without uttering a word to me. When he did speak, he told stories of war, of cold, wet, mud filled trenches, bad food, the blast of bombs, the broken body parts of his fellow soldiers and unbelievable horrors that continued to haunt him throughout the years. He had also an almost irrational dislike, not of the German's he had fought, but the French. Nothing made in France came into our home.

Cecil suffered from what they called neurasthenia, a nervous condition which today would be called Post-Traumatic Stress Disorder (PTSD). Often, I would open a door and be startled to find him standing behind it. My stepfather, a Methodist and teetotaler, had strict requirements in the home, one being that I could only listen to classical music on the radio. The other girls talked of Elvis, Tommy Steele, and the Everley Brothers, but, in my home, my stepfather would not let me hear their music.

When I arrived home from school each evening, mother had gone to work, as a night nurse, and I was alone in the house with a man who seldom, if ever, spoke to me. I was still waiting to go home.

I was miserable at home and used to spend a lot of time at my dancing school or just being out of the house.

Unfortunately, I did not know of another way to leave home so I married and had a child at a young age. My husband was five years older and lived in Birkenhead, hundreds of miles away. The only thing I remember about the wedding in St Anne's Church, Birkenhead, is that the vicar wore dirty shoes.

When my husband drank, he became abusive and after he pushed me down the stairs when I was pregnant, I went to the Birkenhead Police station to file a complaint. They gave me a nice cup of tea and took me back to the house. The police did not want to become involved in domestic problems. Regardless of the extent of abuse, they officially looked the other way. I remember asking him if he would change his ways. When he answered "No" I knew it was time to leave.

I began divorce proceedings at a time and in a country where ending a marriage took at least five years and it was considered shameful to take such action, particularly for a woman. Many English couples did not divorce but lived together in misery because the laws were so strict.

In recent years, a friend told me that a mutual childhood friend's father had committed suicide some years ago. When I asked the reason my friend laughed and said, "He was in an awful marriage for years and he couldn't take it anymore." As a child, I had spent some time with the family and had thought them to be happy together. Obviously, looks were deceiving. Rather than go through the humiliation of a British divorce, this man took his own life. While this was the extreme case, I knew of other couples who for years shared a house but not a life.

Women were often not treated equally in divorce proceedings that were conducted by male judges.

I remember sitting in the solicitor's office on a small chair in front of his big desk. It was an intimidating feeling, but maybe I was too young and determined to let the experience frighten me.

The attitude at the time was, whatever happened, it was the woman's fault. Even abuse was considered the wife's fault. The police would not deal with domestic problems.

I decided then to return with my child to Devon. Possibly because my mother was a strong role model, I knew that women did not have to put up with such behavior. I was nineteen when I chose to put an end to yet another bad situation.

The decree nisi was granted after five years. My child support was thirty shillings a week. (A sum, I should add, that I seldom received.)

My situation illustrates that the country had not moved far from my mother's wartime experience. The value of women, or their children, was not highly regarded.

One day, mother came to collect me from Linton. I was finally, I believed, going home. I would like to say that I remember the trip home and the excitement of that moment but that would be untrue.

However, I can imagine how wonderful it must have been to finally leave Linton and go home with my mother. I know, though, that it must have felt somewhat anti-climactic, because each month when mother visited me I wanted her to take me home. As the months went by, I became numb with disappointment. Each month I was sure she would agree to take me with her and we would live as we had before I went with Reverend Dean to the Methodist School.

For years, I daydreamed of going home after school to find mother there in a warm room with a meal on the table. Unfortunately, that seldom happened after I did go home. The person I called "my real father" was always in that imagined home, but in reality, he never was. Mother never did explain why he was not there.

The experience of being removed from my home with no explanation, and waiting for days, weeks, months, and finally years to go home, caused me to give up hoping. I accepted that adult promises had no meaning. I learned not to trust.

Soon after I left Linton, I went to the Children's Hospital to have my tonsils removed. I remember the huge red balloon they lowered over my face to administer the gas used for the operation and fighting to resist it while the nurse spoke to me in a quiet voice. I had to stay in the hospital for a few days, and no one visited. When it was time to go home the nurse told me that mother would collect me at a certain time. The time came and went, and I was convinced that they would leave me at the hospital for years. I sat on the iron hospital bed and swung my legs back and forth, certain that I would never go home. I gave up believing mother would come and was too upset to appreciate her arrival when she finally did come to collect me.

The result of the experience for me was to mistrust anyone and anything. Even today, I find it hard to accept that people will actually fulfill promises. It is hard to trust when the people you loved the most repeatedly let you down.

Probably as a coping mechanism, I split the world into two. One was an adult world, where they knew everything. The other was the child's world, where you did not know anything. For me, as a child, I had no control. People did things to you, not with you, and with no explanation. No one asked how it felt. I thought adults did not care. I didn't talk with anyone about my feelings--there was no one to talk with. I buried my feelings very deeply and could always put on a smile, a mask that I maintained for years.

I do remember our kind neighbors on the Ravenscliffe estate who welcomed me home. Tom and Ann Hood, a couple who had married late in life, had a daughter named Beryl who was the same age as me. Tom Hood was a big, gruff looking man with a big, hooked nose, who for many years had been the Withernsea, Yorkshire, lighthouse keeper.

Mrs. Hood was a small, intense woman who had a habit of constantly running her fingers through her gray hair as she read the newspaper. Each Sunday, she would invite me to have Yorkshire pudding with sugar on it at their house before I went home to eat my lunch with my mother and stepfather.

Because they were older parents, Beryl used to complain about their old-fashioned ideas. Her mother dressed her in button boots, stylish in Victorian times, that required the use of a buttonhook to fasten the many small buttons. Beryl also wore a cloak that she said made her look like a witch. For an eight-year-old, Beryl had a good sense of humor. "I'm the only girl at my school wearing clothes like these," she would say with a smile. Beryl poked fun at her mother and herself, while wearing her old-fashioned attire without making too much fuss.

Mr. Hood was the caretaker at the Greengates Wesleyan Church. The night before my mother's wedding, I went to the church with Mr. and Mrs. Hood and Beryl. Soon I was following Beryl around the church, the two of us singing "Knees-Up Mother Brown" at the top of our lungs, and banging our knees against large tin trays with each step. The noise was deafening, but no one told us to stop. Beryl's parents were more tolerant of noise than my mother would have been.

The next day, mother and my stepfather were married at the church. Mother wore a blue Harris Tweed suit, which must have taken many clothing coupons. Beryl and I wore long, red velvet dresses with poke bonnets to match. We drove to the church in a taxi -- the first time I had driven in one.

Mother's sister, Annie, was a confectioner, and had made a pale pink three-tier wedding cake with fragile pink fan-shaped trelliswork that billowed out at each corner of the square cakes. I wondered how a person could make such delicate decorations. I had never seen anything like them before and hated to see mother ruin the cake by cutting into it. I was fascinated when mother put pieces of the cake in small silver-and-white boxes with horseshoes and bell shaped decorations, specially made to hold the cake. Mother sent the boxes to friends and family who could not be present. Even in wartime, these small boxes were available.

I do not remember whether my brother came to the wedding, but I do know that he did not come home from Linton to live with us.

After mother married my stepfather, she still worked. Cecil was often ill, and during the winter of 1947, mother trudged through the snow, because there were no buses running, and opened and took care of his shop.

My time at home brought some firsts, like the real egg mother served in the garden of our house in an eggcup shaped like an elephant. This was a treasured memory indeed. How different it tasted from the watery powdered eggs we had at Linton! To this day, an egg seems like a special treat. The other first was a banana, which gave me a bad stomachache.

Going home meant beginning a new life. No more boarding schools, no more bombs... We all hoped for a happy childhood. What none of us evacuees realized was that we would carry the scars of war-time life with us for many years to come.

For the rest of my life I had difficulty with belief in myself. It was my husband of forty years who helped me to trust and to believe in my own abilities.

———————————

I met my husband while I was visiting a friend in Essex and she invited me to go with her to the Officers' Club at Wethersfield Air Force Base, close to her home. I had never met any Americans before. She asked me to go into the club while she parked the car. I walked in the door of the club and a young good-looking man in a civilian suit walked out of one of the small side rooms at precisely that moment. He thrust out his hand, gave me a head-to-toe look that encompassed my long blond hair, navy-blue sleeveless dress and white shoes, and said, "My name is Wayne Lehr."

I met Wayne R. Lehr on 9 July 1960. Unbeknownst to me he was due to be married on 8 August 1960. I later learned that the invitations had gone out, the ring and dress selected, and the groom was due to go to the United States for the wedding within a month of our meeting.

Wayne invited us to have a drink with him and I learned he was a fighter pilot in a US Air Force squadron based at Wethersfield, England. He was a second lieutenant, the lowest officer rank, and due to go on duty at midnight. He explained that he would be going to Libya for three weeks, but could he call me when he returned. I said yes, but doubted that he would make that call. My thinking was to go out with him if only to bring him down a peg or two. He was so bombastic compared with the Englishmen I had known.

Wayne did call me when he returned and came to the house that evening with a bottle of Joy perfume and a dozen red roses. I was more than a little impressed. We had a wonderful dinner and I discovered he was much less overpowering in a one-on-one situation. We began to see each other quite often.

The entire squadron knew that he was due to be married. I did not. One evening a captain's wife, who had a little too much to drink said, "I hope Wayne isn't going to give up his American girl to marry some 'English floosie.'" Obviously, I was the "English floosie." No one else at the table commented and Wayne told me that the woman was drunk. Wayne was a handsome man and I knew he must have had girlfriends so I thought no more about it.

Wayne did not return to the US for the wedding and before the month was out, he had asked me to marry him.

When I met Lloyd Boothby, Wayne's flight commander he said, "My mother told me about you for years and I have finally met you." I wondered what he meant because I had certainly never met him before. He later explained that during the war years his mother continually told him to "clean his plate because the children in Europe were starving."

While this was a simplistic view of the war years, people were hungry, but children could deal with hunger and the bombing of their cities. What they found the most difficult was separation from their parents.

On the steps of Westminster Abbey, one former evacuee, at the 60th Anniversary of the evacuation, said, "I asked my mother when I was older, 'why did you send us away?'"

This woman asked the primary question that has haunted many former evacuees since 1 September 1939. Even after 70 years, it is the question they would most like answered.

Inwardly, I asked the same question, but never voiced it to anyone. I loved my mother but I seemed unable to have a close relationship with her.

Why would a child trust someone who sent him or her to live with strangers when he or she was too young to understand the reason? Why would a child trust someone who did not tell her that her father had died? Had anyone taken the time to explain why these things, and others like them, had happened, it would have made life easier for thousands of evacuees.

Contemporary British parents, when told about the WWII evacuation invariably comment, "How could parents send their children away?" In hindsight and not having to worry about the fear of a German invasion or being bombed out of their homes, this choice is easy to make. With the British social programs that began shortly after WWII that many argue are the direct result of the evacuation, today's parents are provided with safety nets that wartime parents could only dream about.

Unfortunately, things happened to the children and seldom were they explained. The parents, and in this case, the government decided the where and the when of any explanations. Many of the evacuees said they would have appreciated someone to explain their situation to, someone to go to when things were not good. Although the staff at Linton tried to do this, each one had the impossible task of listening to the wants of 50 children. That in itself was a full-time job.

The communications of the 1930s and 1940s were newspapers, magazines, newsreels at the cinema, and the radio if a family could afford one. The progress of the war came through these media and, unlike today, our parents had no way to check on the accuracy of those details.

In some instances, the teachers prevented the parents from entering the schools as the children gathered prior to leaving for their evacuation journeys. The authorities thought they knew better and the parents would be disruptive to their plans for an orderly evacuation.

I was fortunate that mother was able to take me herself, on a visiting day, to the Linton school. This was probably an arrangement mother made with Mr. Sternwhite because I was to be the youngest child in the school. I have no idea how my brother went to Linton originally. Usually, Ailsa went to pick up the children in Bradford and escort them to Linton.

The evacuation was not compulsory. For parents it may have been easier for them if it had been. History shows that it was their decision for their children to leave their homes. When the evacuation experience was positive, they received the praise, but for those children who had negative experiences the blame was life-long.

Problems of concern to the parents who did evacuate their children included the possibility of losing the children's affection to another "mother." They worried about losing control of their children and thought that their sons and daughters would "forget" them. How would they be able to communicate with the children? Some of the children were not old enough to write.

Winifred remembers parents who went to Linton and said the child was "homesick or ill" because of the separation from the family. In many cases, it turned out that the parent could not cope with the loss of the child.

When the bombs began to fall in 1940 many parents became more convinced that they should send their children away from what they realized was a dangerous situation. Mary Manley's parents did not consider sending her away until a bomb dropped close to their home.

When people have not experienced danger, they think it cannot happen to them. The day, they realized that what they considered a safe situation is no longer and bombs could drop on their homes, their thinking changes.

More parents showed a willingness to send their children away in the autumn of 1940 after the Battle of Britain and Dunkirk than they had in 1939. War became real – not something they read about in the newspapers.

The British knew that the Germans had occupied Holland, Belgium, and France in the summer of 1940. Shortly thereafter, the Channel Islands, British Crown dependencies (Guernsey, Jersey, Alderney, Salk) also fell under German rule. The only British territory occupied by the Germans in WW II. Prior to the invasion, the British Navy rescued thousands of the islanders.

It was on these British ships that the Cleels and the Gallienne boys came to England and then to the Linton school. How strange and frightening it must have been for these children to be so far from their parents.

With German occupation of their homeland a certainty, how difficult it must have been for German parents or Channel Island parents to part with their children. No-one knew how bad life would be under German occupation. Those children who went to England at least survived. The Channel Island children did not go home until after the British sent war ships to the islands on 8 May1945. Most of the German Jewish children had no home or family to return to when the war ended.

Today's parents can reflect on how they felt when their child went off to school for the first time, or when that same grown child left home for good. We talk about the empty nest syndrome. These parents often receive sympathy. We can only imagine the anguish of those men and women who evacuated their children believing they were saving their lives.

Until the last twenty years, there was little in the literature about WW II evacuees. Their parents had less information written about them and their reactions to the evacuation. Reading accounts of the three waves of evacuations in 1939, 1940 and 1944, seldom are parents mentioned except to say that there were "weeping mothers" along the roadway.

In wartime even we children were told not to cry. The Evacuee song, "Goodnight Children Everywhere" tells the children, "Don't be a wimp or a weeping willow." So for adults, although it was difficult for the mothers not to shed tears, it was acceptable when they saw the children leave. For the men it was not. In many instances, they had already left to serve in the war, but those who didn't seemed to avoid the problem by staying at home. While at the time, it was acceptable for women to shed tears, men did not cry.

In one account, a child speaks about how her father would not come downstairs to say goodbye. She saw him in the window looking "rather odd," his face blocked by the curtain. At a time when men found it hard to express their emotions, the loss of a beloved child had to be heart-wrenching.

How much worse it must have been for parents to see their children, ages one to fifteen sent away to unknown destinations. Parents of evacuated children did not know their children's destinations. Those evacuation trains did not have a listed itinerary any more than did the troop trains.

Ruth Inglis, in her 1989 book, *The Children's War*, said, "Evacuees were a proud, independent group." I agree with her. Any child sent away from family, friends and all that is familiar, at a young age, had to be independent. When you had to make your own decisions on all aspects of life, from such an early age, independence had to be second nature to all evacuees. I learned at a young age to make my own decisions and to take care of myself.

Mary Manley spoke about how her parents, particularly her mother found it hard to deal with her independence when she went home. In the intervening years everything had changed, the parents and their children.

The research for this book was not easy on any level. It is difficult to shine a light on a past you have spent a lifetime forgetting. It took more than twenty years for me to reach a place where I could speak about my childhood experiences. And it took many more years before I could write about the things I discovered.

I felt it important enough to examine and write about a lost childhood. What did I learn about myself from the detective work? What did I learn about my mother? What did I learn about the separation of children from their parents? What is my verdict on the British evacuation? Why did the British government not feel it necessary to conduct research to question what affect the evacuation had on those one and half million children? More importantly, what affect did the evacuation have on evacuees?

We cannot nor should we judge WWII parents through the lens of Britain's welfare state that now provides from the cradle to the grave. We need to view them through the prism of the 1930s and 1940s. To do otherwise is to judge them at a distinct and unfair disadvantage.

Today's parents do not fear they will go hungry if they cannot work. They have numerous social programs to protect them if they lose their jobs.

It was the recognition of the poverty of some evacuee children sent away without adequate clothing and shoes to their host families during the evacuation that pressured by the British government to put those social programs that everyone today takes for granted, into effect.

The National Health Service is a result of the British government's recognition that children needed nutritious food in anticipation of the shortages of war. In wartime, the government began to allocate orange juice, malt and cod-liver oil and milk for children. In the early 1940s when the Germans blockaded and bombed provision ships, the country came to a point where people were hungry. We children at Linton could vouch for that – if not hungry, we were certainly bored to death, with spam and tapioca, (hence the strike).

Wartime parents did what they could with the information they had. Given the lack of communication and the difficulty of their decisions, we should congratulate rather than condemn these men and women for their sacrifices and for their courage.

My husband was one of the most positive people I have ever met. If asked how he felt he regularly answered, "Fantastic." Friends and colleagues nicknamed him "Mr. Fantastic." Even when he was in the last few months of his life, his answer was always the same.

Wayne was the one who encouraged me to further my education, to achieve and to write the book.

PHOTO ALBUM

Mother, Jessie
Elizabeth Drewry

Father,
Walter Drewry

Uncle Howard Lowe,
prior to leaving
England in 1940
for the Middle East
returning after the
war in 1945

Doreen
before
evacuation

Brother, Keith,
six years of age, at
63 Blackstone Ave.,
Wyke.

Doreen with Beryl
Hood, bridesmaids at
her mother's wedding
at Greengates
Wesleyan Church,
1944

Linton Headmaster,
Mr. Sternwhite and
teacher Mrs. Ellison,
taking tea with the
girls, Mary Manley
and Rosie Goy
sitting in front.

Linton Residential
School, Yorkshire,
built for evacuees
and opened on
10 July 1940.

PART TWO

A BIGGER PICTURE

◇◇

S ometimes, the strongest bonds aren't produced by love—or even by hatred—but by shared experiences, by having seen and known the world in a way that few others can understand or appreciate. The difficult process I have gone through to capture the hidden details of my own life is a process others have lived. Everyone's life is unique, but many of us from that time and that place are tied to this shared moment in our childhoods. Those who have lived through this won't need an explanation of why this is so important. But others may.

1. LOOKING FOR CONTEXT

I certainly felt a need to connect my story to a wider community, so I sought out others who could help me provide a deeper context for the narrow range of my own memories and those whom I knew in earlier days.

I started with a 2009 conversation[25] with James Roffey, the man who began the Evacuee Reunion Association (ERA). James told me why he felt compelled to create a support organization for former evacuees.

His inspiration came in 1989, just prior to the 50th WWII Anniversary, when he wrote a letter to then-Prime Minister John Major asking if WWII evacuees would be included in the observances and parade.

One of Major's young aides telephoned and asked James, "What exactly are evacuees?" He said he knew "a few hundred poor children from the inner cities were sent to the countryside," and wondered if that is what James meant.

The comment infuriated James. He said, "Young man, there were millions of evacuees, and we weren't all poor children from the slums." To make sure he never had to have a conversation like that again, James formed the ERA to give WWII evacuees a voice, to make them visible and to change the negative stereotypes that had been perpetrated through British literature and media.

John Major's young aide certainly was not alone in his ignorance of WWII evacuees, however. The myths and outright falsehoods surrounding the evacuation are staggering and continue to the present time. A former evacuee wrote in the August 1998 edition of the ERA magazine[26] that at a Weymouth WWII ceremony in July of that year, a Women's Land Army member continually harassed former evacuees, saying they had not been bombed or machine-gunned and they therefore had no right to march in the parade. The fact that this war veteran, who also had not fought, believed that children had not made a sacrifice equal to her own, was troubling. It suggested that most people believed that the true story of the evacuation happened in the way the government portrayed it in their wartime propaganda in the media and cinema newsreels—and in many books and films since. These portrayals may have been necessary for the morale of the country, during wartime. But a more accurate portrayal could have been told to the British public, post-war, in schools and in media stories.[27]

The evacuations were not exactly secret. They involved millions of people. The evacuation scheme was planned and implemented in 1939 by an Evacuation sub-committee of the Imperial Defence Committee and had been formulated as early as 16 February 1931 in order to prevent panic and to "create an orderly exodus from London [and other cities] in the event of war." Sir John Anderson formed an evacuation committee whose mission was to put children, the future of the country, out of the range of aerial attacks.

The war with Germany began in September 1939 and ended in May 1945. During those five years and eight months, there were three large government-organized evacuations. 1 September 1939 is a date forged into the memories of thousands of British WW II evacuees. On that day, with the words, "Evacuate Forthwith," and fearing a bombing attack from the German Luftwaffe, 1,475,500 people—including 99,000 mothers and children, and 62,000 children in school parties— left their city homes for the presumed safety of the countryside.[28]

Dr. Martin Parsons, Director of the Research Centre for Evacuee and War Child Studies at the University of Reading, in his 1998 book *I'll Take That One*, included *The Dorset Daily Echo* headline from 1 September 1939: "Greatest Evacuation in History Has Begun…Three Million People on the Move".

"Even the exodus of the Bible – the flight of the Israelites from Egypt – is dwarfed into insignificance by comparison," the *Echo's* reporter wrote.[29]

However, after this huge exodus, the expected bombing attacks didn't take place. Thousands of evacuees began to drift home, much to the distress of the government, who knew that the expected bombing was only a matter of time.

The second evacuation began with the Battle of Britain, when the severe bombing convinced 1,250,000 individuals—141,000 of whom were unaccompanied children—to again leave the cities for the countryside.

The third evacuation came in 1944 when the Germans launched pilotless planes called Doodlebugs, armed with VI missiles, against Britain's civilian population. They were followed by the even more destructive V-2 missiles in a series of attacks that lasted until May 1945, just prior to the end of the war.

During the second and third evacuations, the severity of the bombing convinced families that their children would be safer away from the cities. The parents who sent their children away to friends and to family did not always use government evacuations. This made it difficult for the government to keep accurate data on the movement and actual number of people evacuated.

2. INVISIBLE WITNESSES

Research difficulties notwithstanding, a few people have taken the time to research the facts and challenge the evacuation myths—for example, that all evacuees were ill-mannered, dirty, lice-ridden, diseased individuals from the slums who had no place in decent society. A more sensitive researcher would have concluded that the children, wrenched suddenly from everything familiar, used as servants for host families were lonely, confused and unhappy, and, in some extreme cases, abused. Their mothers were similarly disparaged as lazy and slovenly with few, if any, mothering or culinary skills. These women left their homes seeking refuge from the danger of the cities, often sharing a home and a kitchen with the hostess. City evacuee mothers left the cacophony of traffic and street markets, cheery vendors loudly peddling their wares, welcoming pubs, and lifelong friends on every corner. For those women, rural villages and towns must have felt as lively as graveyards. In many instances, the host families turned these women out with their children each day after breakfast and would not let them return until evening.

Lady Reading, Head of the Women's Voluntary Service, gave a perfect example of the misunderstanding of upper-class women about evacuee mothers and children who came from all strata of British society. "Evacuees," she said, "would be quite happy to live in barns and garages in the countryside, especially if they were next door to a middle class house."[30]

In the film *Hope and Glory*, the children went to live with their grandparents, in idyllic isolation surrounded by family. That may have happened to the director and writer, John Boorman, but not to most evacuees. [31]

Barbara Birchall, for example, recalls, in *Goodnight Children Everywhere*, being evacuated at age three to Reading, Berkshire, with her sister, then age four:

"We went to a lady and her husband who had one daughter. They owned a shoe mender's shop. They were nice people, we thought. But after a couple of years they were very cruel to us. They never fed us much....My father was in Alamein... he used to send us jars of sweets but we never got any...One night we were so hungry and thirsty that we crept downstairs to find something to eat and drink. We couldn't find anything. We were desperate, so I saw the tap was dripping and it made a pool of water in the bottom of the bowl, my sister pulled up a chair to the sink and helped me up...Then I bent my head down and got some of the water in my hand to drink. Then we heard footsteps coming and the woman caught us. She opened the coal cupboard, and pushed us in and locked the door. We had to stay there till the morning. And it was very dark, cold and spiders! Horrible! We were very scared.

If she was cross with us, she used to lock us in the garden shed at the bottom of the garden all night. It was really a nightmare.

My sister had irons up her legs and couldn't walk very well, so I used to take her to school and we were so hungry and sick that we used to sit by the pig swill bins and wait for the rubbish to be thrown away. Then we used to eat as much as we could out of the bins. One day we had a big harvest festival and in the front row was fruit and vegetables and these big tomatoes. We were all sitting on the floor quiet when my sister made a mad dash and took a big bite out of the tomato. The teacher took her and spanked her on the knuckles with a ruler. When I explained that we were very hungry, she called us liars and got the woman round who looked after us, and she denied we were not fed. When we got home she beat us and her husband beat us and we were very afraid that we would die if we didn't get out of there." [32]

Although WWII articles, even today, define wartime Britain as a place full of happy, cheerful individuals enjoying life despite the war, the truth may be closer to the account of former evacuee Bernard Kops, giving a child's reality of war in his book *The World is a Wedding:*

And we went underground to get away from the sirens and the bombs.
Yet they followed me and I heard sirens until the world became a siren.
One endless cry of torture. It penetrated right into the core of my being,
one long siren, a long wail of despair. Some people feel a certain nostalgia
for those days, recall a poetic dream about the blitz. They talk about those
days as if they were a time of a true communal spirit. Not to me. It was
the beginning of an era of utter terror, of fear and horror. I stopped being
a child and came face to face with the new reality of the world. [33]

Allan Burnett, a former evacuee from a middle-class family, eloquently explains how he arrived at his host family's home in Leicestershire after a daylong train journey from London:

At our destination we were herded, hundreds of us, into a school. We were tired, hungry, and irritable, and nobody seemed to know what was happening or who was responsible for what. After a while, we were aware that our numbers were shrinking as people gradually disappeared. There was a touch of Noah's Ark about it....St. Pancras seemed so distant, millennia away in time and space. Eventually we were shepherded on to a Stone Age single decker omnibus, a wheezing coughing contraption protesting volubly at the late night passengers. I presume the bossy lady with the clipboard and Joyce Grenfell accent was the billeting officer.

We were deposited in a seventeenth century farmhouse with as much livestock inside as out. We were hardly welcome, but none of us had any choice in the matter. London met Leicestershire head on. Chalk and cheese.

Our hosts had never seen a tramcar, escalator, department store or even a lavatory chain. The privy was at the end of the garden and designed for two, so at least there was no waiting....We had exchanged electric light, a gas stove, a modern fireplace, a vacuum cleaner and flush toilets for oil lamps a smoky kitchen range, filthy brooms, and bucket sanitation in the middle of nowhere reminiscent of Hansel and Gretel. We coexisted in mutual misunderstanding. [34]

Allan Burnett's experience indicates that not all the evacuees were city children from the slums. His account also shows how little children knew about what to expect when they arrived at their host family homes. The receiving hosts knew nothing of the lives or type of children they would live with for months—or, in many instances, years. Life would have been much easier if these children had been informed about their new surroundings before they suddenly moved from the cities they knew to the countryside they did not.

James Roffey said he had recently encountered an essay written by a British schoolteacher about the evacuation in which she wrote that teachers put labels on the evacuees complete with the children's names and their destinations. They were not; like so much else written and reported on this subject, that was wrong, too. As James later told me, "If British schoolteachers are writing false information about WWII, we have little chance of the next generation learning the correct facts."[35]

The first evacuation of individuals from one place to another went off with great organizational efficiency. Miss Florence Hosborough, at the time an MP and under-secretary for Health, watched the entraining at London Bridge Station. "Everything is going like clockwork," said Miss Horsborough. [36]

Unfortunately, the evacuation committee gave little thought to the fact that these were people, not goods, they were transporting. Consequently, they failed to address the sensibilities and needs of those confused and helpless people, primarily children, they moved so efficiently. The journeys were several hours long and there were no toilets on the trains. The government also gave little thought to what would happen when these efficiently moved women and children arrived at their destinations.

In May 2006, Dr. Martin Parsons said, "One of the most interesting things about children in wartime is that they are the invisible victims." He conducted an experiment with his students and showed them a series of ten photographs each of which contained children in war zones. Only two of the eighteen students said the common denominator in the photographs was children. When we look at war literature, film, or television coverage the focus is seldom on the children who may be present but are usually unseen." [37]

Evacuees and their families were encouraged to "forget" the evacuation once the war was over. It was a reversal from the extensive government wartime propaganda via radio, newspapers, and magazines. The government considered wartime parents patriotic if they sent their children away. The same government paid little attention to those patriotic parents or their evacuated children once the war had ended.

It was only after approximately fifty years that the silence has been broken as some former evacuees began to relate their experiences. When I began to write this book and spoke with old school friends about my evacuee experience, they were shocked. People who had known me since I was ten years old had no idea I had been an evacuee. Mother would tell people I had been at a boarding school and her denial about the evacuation ensured my silence. Only 25 years later was I able to speak about those wartime years. James Roffey told me that even today many former evacuees tell him they have never talked to anyone about their evacuation experience.

When evacuees began to write, or were interviewed about their stories, they presented more realistic accounts. The words of former evacuees reveal truths which previously had been ignored. Similarly, middle- and upper-class former evacuees contradicted the evacuee stereotypes and myths of them being only inner-city slum children. It also broke the silence that had allowed those misconceptions to flourish unchallenged.

Given the examples of the Prime Minister's aide, the contemporary British schoolteacher's essay and the British government's refusal to acknowledge them, it is obvious that the evacuees themselves have had to break that silence and validate their experiences. James Roffey's formation of the ERA has been an excellent example, as has the work of the researchers courageous and patient enough to study a previously "invisible and ignored group of individuals."

The invisibility of evacuees is nothing new. It took fifty years for them to come forward and begin to tell their stories about the evacuation. Since WWII ended, neither Tory nor Labour governments have acknowledged either the evacuees or the evacuation. At the 60th Anniversary at Westminster Abbey, Prime Minister Tony Blair did not send a representative, nor did he want the Royal Family to attend.

The current government under Gordon Brown has so far refused to recognize WWII evacuees with a memorial, or with individual certificates of recognition. It is much easier for a government to deal with a silent, invisible group than to make them visible with official recognition.

3. CHIMNEYSWEEPS AND CHILD MINERS

The practice of "abandoning" British children was not a new concept in 1939. There have been many examples from British history that parallel the wartime evacuations and harsh treatment of children. Ivy Pinchbeck and Margaret Hewitt, in their book *Children in English Society, Vol, 2*, wrote that in pre-industrial and industrial Britain, the idea of children was that they were "little adults"…and "little attempt was made to soften life for them." [38]

Without birth control, women of the 1800s and well into the 1900s had multiple births with high mortality rates. In poor families, another baby was not a source of joy, but rather another mouth to feed. Children's deaths from disease and starvation were common. Many orphaned children ended up fending for themselves on the streets of inhospitable cities. Others went into workhouses or orphanages where their treatment often equaled that depicted by Charles Dickens in *Oliver Twist*.

By 1876, in America some of the states had already passed laws that provided protection for children. British legislators proposed similar laws in 1889 but they failed to pass. It was only in 1933, just six years prior to the outbreak of World War II, that Parliament passed the Children and Young Persons Act to provide safeguards for British children.[39] Before that time, parents and guardians could, and did, abuse children without fear of prosecution.

During the Industrial Revolution and continuing long afterward, working class youth—at least those who survived a childhood of poverty, cold, disease, and scarcity of clothing and food—became part of the work force. British children as young as five years old, went to work in factories and coalmines. Children often learned wage-earning skills at the age of four.[40]

The despair of Tom, Charles Kingsley's protagonist in *The Water Babies*,[41] highlighted the plight of child chimney sweeps in the 1800s, young boys who frequently died of suffocation, fell to their deaths, or became lost in the numerous chimneys of large houses. Kingsley's book brought the public's attention and outrage at the harsh use of boy chimney sweeps, or "climbing boys." Master sweeps often rounded up orphan boys or bought boys small enough to fit into chimneys from poor parents. The boys were given little food, so they would remain small.

"The Chimney Sweeper," written by William Blake in 1789, captures the chilling abuse of climbing boys, their heartbreak and their desperation:

> When my mother died I was very young,
> And my father sold me while yet my tongue,
> Could scarcely cry "Weep, weep, weep, weep!"
> So your chimney I sweep, and in soot I sleep.
>
> There's little Tom Dacre, who cried when his head,
> That curled like a lamb's back, was shaved; so I said,
> Hush, Tom! Never mind it, for, when your head's bare,
> You know that the soot cannot spoil your white hair."
>
> And so he was quiet, and that very night,
> As Tom was a-sleeping, he had such a sight!—
> That thousands of sweepers, Dick, Joe, Ned, and Jack,
> Were all of them locked up in coffins of black.

And by came an angel who had a bright key,
And he opened the coffins and let them all free;
Then down a green plain, leaping, laughing, they run,
And wash in a river, and shine in the sun.

Then naked and white, all their bags left behind,
They rise upon clouds, and sport in the wind;
And the Angel told Tom, if he'd be a good boy,
He'd have God for his father, and never want joy.

And so Tom awoke, and we rose in the dark,
And we got our bags and our brushes to work,
Though the morning was cold, Tom was happy and warm;
So if all do their duty they need not fear harm. [42]

Blake's poem was a harsh criticism of a society that still allowed children as young as four years old to be exploited and abused for financial gain. Blake's writing, like that of Kingsley, attempted to raise awareness about the cruel reality of these children's lives. They attempted to prick the societal conscience. The result was a gradual, if slow, control of the practice of using small children to sweep the nation's chimneys.

In 1788, The British Parliament passed the Act for the Better Regulation of Chimney Sweepers and Their Apprentices. The act limited a sweeper to six apprentices no younger than eight years old. Unfortunately, the act was seldom enforced. Parliament finally passed the Act for the Regulation of Chimney Sweeps in 1864. The law banned the practice of using climbing boys as chimney sweeps. Unlike the concern many had for British middle-class children, few cared about the welfare of these poor young boys and their miserable lives. Like war-children, they too were invisible.

4. 350 YEARS OF 'WAIFS'

We might question why a government, which planned the WWII evacuation so carefully, did not research the benefits or the problems that resulted from this huge social experiment. The answer could be because it was not the first British government involvement in a large-scale scheme that separated parents and children.

For centuries, the British government had kept silent on the emigration, both legally and illegally, of thousands of children. The British government and the recipient countries, Australia, Canada, New Zealand and Rhodesia, also kept their silence.

The first official involuntary—that is, without the consent of either families or the children—migration of children happened in 1619 when 100 vagrant British children were illegally rounded up and dispatched to Virginia. The final contingent of children thus expelled from Britain left in 1967 when Barnados flew nine children from Britain to Australia. These were the last British children given over to different secular and religious organizations and "evacuated" from their old lives into a new country and a new life.

In 1945, the population of Australia was only seven million people. Consequently, the Australians held a conference to outline a plan to populate their country. "Far from being passive recipients of British children, the Australian Government actively sought 'Good White Stock' to protect Australia by building the population as quickly and cheaply as possible…The present proposal, approved in principle by the Commonwealth Governments on whose full co-operation its success depends, is for an official child migration scheme….It is proposed that the Commonwealth Government seek out in Britain and Europe, in each of the first three post-war years, at least 17,000 children a year [i.e., About 50,000 in three years] suitable for migration to Australia." [43]

The records are poor; we don't even know the number of children involved. To quote a 2001 Child Migrant report: "Even today, nobody in the Australian or British Governments can give an accurate number of how many children arrived in Australia… This is not a piece of ancient history -- it happened in the 20th Century. That there is no clarity of this important issue is a good example of the lack of attention to detail that illustrates the Governments' administration of the Schemes." [44]

Many of these children, falsely labeled orphans, had no idea of their identities. Perry Snow, a Canadian clinical psychologist, in *Neither Waif Nor Stray: The Search For a Stolen Identity*,[45] about his father, Frederick George Snow, who in 1913, was made a ward of an organization then called the "Church of England Incorporated Society for Providing Homes for Waifs and Strays"—but more conveniently known today as The Children's Society. Snow was just four years old when put into care. The child lived a loveless institutional life in England when, with thousands of other children also called "Waifs," was told at age 15 that he was no longer wanted in Britain and given the option of moving to Australia or Canada. He chose Canada. Children sent to those countries were between the ages of six and fifteen. The majority of them did not go to families, but to religious institutions. While some children had good treatment, the majority encountered conditions that in some cases were horrendous.

The institutions stripped the children of their identities because unidentified children were easier to transport to other countries. Today few of the institutions mention in their histories their involvement in child migration. Perry Snow said that the organization refused to open their records to his father during his lifetime. After 55 years of attempting to discover the facts about his life, George Snow died in 1994 without knowing about his family or his real identity.

Most organizations deliberately isolated children from their families. Dr. John Barnado went to trial 88 times for kidnapping children because he claimed that their parents were "evil associations." Although found guilty of the charges, Barnado continued to send children out of the country without the parents' permission.

And why not? Canada, Australia, Rhodesia and New Zealand all needed "good white stock" to populate their countries. Through the years, religious organizations in Britain—including the Church of England, Catholic Charities, the Salvation Army and Dr. Barnados, along with others—were instrumental in child migration. British orphanages overflowing with poor children were happy to supply these countries with "orphans." The receiving country often paid for each child, and, for a double benefit, the British institution was relieved of the expense of feeding and clothing them. The British Child Emigration Scheme involved fifty child-care organizations who transported 100,000 children to Canada from 1880-1930. Interrupted only by World War I and World War II, the Canadian scheme continued until the mid-1960s. The organizations professed to be sending the children overseas to give them better lives. Whether they were successful or not is a subject for debate.

"Home Children" or "Waifs" were just some of the names used to refer to the Canadian child migrants. British Home Children were constantly labeled "worthless" by their caretakers, and treated accordingly. The majority received no payment when they worked fourteen to sixteen hours a day, six days a week, on farms or as laborers on building sites.[46]

Most child migrants did not go to school or have adequate medical care, and had little to no protection under the law. Once in these foreign countries the British organizations that sent the children did not oversee their treatment. A reputed half of these children suffered from child neglect and abuse. "The children were commodities," Snow wrote, "deported because they were unwanted in Britain." When they were eighteen years old, turned out into the world to fend for themselves the child migrants had no identities, little education and few skills.

"My father never had a birth certificate," wrote Snow. "He had nothing to verify who he was for the first 33 years of his life…he had serious doubts if his name was really Snow."

In 1995, a Public Broadcasting Services (PBS) announcer began a film called *The Orphan Trains*[47] with the words: "Tonight on The American Experience – some were orphans, some lived on the streets, others were merely poor. All would be sent far away….One sure measure of the heart and soul of any society is how it treats its children."

"In the 1850s, in New York City, thousands of homeless children prowled the streets in search of money, food, and shelter. Their families came from rural America and Europe looking for work. The crowded tenements were subject to outbreaks of disease and the depressing lifestyle to alcohol abuse. The plight of these impoverished children became an obsession of a young minister, Charles Loring Brace. He was horrified by what he saw on the streets. As he wandered through the city, he talked with children, recording their stories in his diary. He discovered young children sent on the streets to beg for money, young girls sweeping the crosswalks and older girls prostituting themselves." [48]

In 1853, Brace founded the Children's Aid Society and, no doubt, had intended to improve the lives of children by rescuing them from the slums of New York. Brace understood the need for labor in the expanding farm country and thought rural families would be happy to take these "orphan" children. Brace believed that "the best of all asylums for the outcast life is to get these children of unhappy fortune utterly out of their surroundings and to send them away to kind Christian homes in the country."[49] Three times a month agents of the Society assembled the children into groups ranging from six to one hundred and fifty.[50]

In local newspapers notices ran in advance, encouraging people to come see the homeless children on the stage of a meeting hall. As the children waited to be displayed, they were urged to make a good impression on the audience.[51] Those children not chosen in one town were put on the train to try their luck in the next town.

Denis Boyles wrote in his book *Superior, Nebraska* that "between 1853 and 1930 the United States brought more than 200,000 children from the crowded, filthy alleys of New York, where at any given moment as many as 30,000 homeless children roamed the streets, to new homes in spacious places like rural Kansas and Nebraska."[52] While most of those children went to private homes, according to Boyles, some "were treated as indentured labor and given little affection or education." Luck was on the side of some of the children; there are letters and first-hand oral confirmations saying things such as, "I will always be grateful for what I was given." Nebraska retiree Ann Harrison, one of the last surviving Orphan Train children, told Boyles if she had not been taken from her New York home, "I can't imagine what would have happened to me."

The parents had few options when they were sick or had lost a spouse. Signing over the children to the Children's Aid Society was often the only way out of a dire situation. Many of the children remembered their fathers or mothers crying as they left on the trains to go to Indiana, Kansas, Michigan, Mississippi, Nebraska, Texas, and other rural states. The migrant children worried that the southerners who had recently lost their slaves wanted the orphan train children to replace them. Other people wanted children, both male and female, to clean their homes or work in the fields. Did the parents of these "orphans," taken by the hundreds from the cities to live in those rural states, know the children were leaving, and had they given their permission?

These children left all that was familiar to live with strangers. Some children went to good homes—and some did not. "The record books are filled with names and dates, details of departures and arrivals, but say little about the quality of the children's treatment. The extent of abuse is unknown." One young girl wrote how when she left on the train her father gave her a pink envelope with his address written on it. When she awoke the following morning, the envelope was missing. The child never saw the envelope, her only link with her father, again. The female caretaker she asked about it said, "You won't need the envelope where you are going."

Another young woman wrote the following letter to the Children's Aid Society from Elkhart, Indiana, on May 28th 1865.

Dear Friend: The place where I lived I did not like. They whipped me till I was all black and blue. I told the lady I did not like to stay there, so she told me I might leave. I have a good place now. I hope you will write to me and let me know if you see any of my folks in New York. I would give one hundred worlds like this if I could see my mother. Kate Murphy. (9)

Kate Murphy's mother died without the comfort of having her daughter with her, or even knowing where she had gone.

In 1986, Margaret Humphreys, a Nottingham social worker and mother of two, received a letter from a woman who said at age four, in the post-war period, the British government sent her on a boat to Australia. Margaret Humphreys did not think this account could possibly be true. However, to her astonishment, further investigation revealed that the British government between 1922 and 1967 had shipped not one child, but thousands of children from a variety of orphanages and children's homes to help populate the white outposts of the British Empire.

In post-war Britain, when a family could not provide for their families from loss of job or illness or other social problems, they could not afford to keep their children. These families had no option but to turn to children's homes or orphanages to place their children, sometimes for a short period of time until their situations improved. Families put their children into Dr. Barnados, Catholic Child Welfare Council, The Children's Society, the Church of England and other religious institutions with known and trusted reputations. In these institutions, many children had been orphaned by the war, but not all. Estimates of the number of British children sent to Australia between 1947 and 1967 vary between five thousand and ten thousand.

The Child Migrants' Trust, founded by Margaret Humphreys, reported to the British House of Commons Health Committee in 1997, "We have received many examples of children wrongly being told that their parents were dead." (Parents who went to collect their children were told British families had adopted them when in fact they had been shipped abroad.) Given this information by adults they trusted, the children had no reason to doubt their word. Enticed by stories about an exciting boat trip to a wonderful new country the children, too young to understand, went on these long sea journeys to their new countries. The majority of these children, many as young as five years old, were falsely labeled orphans.

Most went to Australian charitable and religious institutions. While not all the children involved in the scheme suffered abuse, many lived through almost unbelievable brutality. Allegations of the systematic rape of children surfaced in 1996 against the Christian Brothers, at their orphanages like the infamous Bindoon in Western Australia. "The history of child migration in Australia is in many ways a history of cruelty, lies and deceit," wrote Bean and Mellville. [53]

As the Trust reported, "After being told fanciful tales of travel to the 'Land of Milk and Honey' where children ride to school on horseback and pick up fruit on the side of the road, child migrants were sent to Australia without passports, social histories or even the most basic documentation about their identities." [54]

Many of the migrants Humphreys interviewed told of severe beatings, child labor and pedophilia, which a 1997 United Kingdom, House of Commons report described as "quite exceptional depravity so that terms like 'sexual abuse' are too weak to convey it." [55]

The child migrant scheme brought to the attention of the Australian and British governments by Margaret Humphrey's[56] investigations shocked the people of both countries who had no idea that such things had taken place in the not-too-distant past.

Although the Australian and the British governments had hearings on the child migration scheme, neither had investigated the subject prior to Humphrey's revelations. Although successive post-war British governments took advantage of parents who could not provide for their children and gave them to the Australian government to boost population or to provide labor, they do not feel it necessary to apologize to the former child migrants.

Both the evacuation and the child migrant schemes—as is the case for many similar schemes over hundreds of years—were purported to be "in the best interest of the children." John Hennessey, who was 10 when he was sent to Australia in 1947, told an Australian Parliamentary Inquiry in 1998 that he was stripped naked and flogged almost to death by a Christian Brother for stealing grapes from a vineyard in Western Australia. In 1993, the Christian Brothers issued a public apology for the abuses they admitted had taken place at their child-care institutions.[57] In 1996, former migrants whose lives were shattered by the treatment they received in those Catholic orphanages received an out of court settlement of $5.1 million from the Christian Brothers.[58]

5. ORPHANS AND 'SAVIORS'

The International Association of Former Child Migrants and Their Families (IAFCMTF), in their 2001 Australian Senate Community Affairs References Committee Submission, attempted to set the record straight on child migrants and deal with the many myths associated with their deportation. In the report, the child migrants who make up the IAFCMTF set the record straight on one of the major myths, namely that the children sent by social agencies to Australia were "war orphans and unwanted street urchins."

While there may have been a few orphans, the overwhelming majority of children had mothers, fathers, and extended families in the United Kingdom when they were deported. This cruel lie stopped the majority from ever searching for their parents and families; or asking for records. Why would you search for your parents when you have been told they are dead?

To label us unwanted street urchins was despicable and untrue. It stigmatizes former Child Migrants and our families. It is also highly disrespectful to our mothers and fathers, many of whom came to claim us but were similarly deceived by Churches and charities who lied that we had been adopted in England - or often in America.

Children were sought for deportation directly from children's homes in Britain, and from their own families by stealth. The Australian and British Governments worked in partnership with Churches and charities to round up children in a planned and organized strategy. [59]

Unfortunately, myths repeated for generations take on a life of their own and become part of the common lexicon. The report mentions what the Child Migrants considered the flawed research of Alan Gill's 1997 book entitled *Orphans of the Empire: The Shocking Story of Child Migration to Australia.*

The Child Migrant report explains, "The term 'Orphan' is highly emotive. It was used in the propaganda of the governments and the deporting agencies to exploit public sympathy and the public purse and to promote them as 'saviors' of vulnerable 'unwanted' orphan children. It is now widely acknowledged that the overwhelming majority of former Child Migrants were not orphans."[60]

Similarly, just as the majority of Child Migrants were not orphans, the majority of evacuees were not from poor working-class families.

On 16 November 2009, UK Guardian reporter Adam Gabbatt wrote that Kevin Rudd, the Australian prime minister, issued an emotional apology to the surviving British children who were forcibly shipped to Australia during the last century. "We are sorry" he said. "Sorry that, as children, you were taken from your families and placed in institutions where you were so often abused. Sorry for the physical suffering, the emotional starvation and the absence of love, of tenderness, of care."

Government records show that at least 150,000 children aged between three and 14 were sent to Commonwealth countries, mainly Australia and Canada, in a programme that began in the 1920s and did not end until 1967.

The children – the majority of whom were already in some form of social or charitable care – were cut off from their families and even falsely informed that they were orphans.

Parents were told the children had gone to a better life, but many of them ended up in institutions or were sent to work unpaid on farms, with many facing abuse.

Bonnie Malkin, of the British Telegraph reported that, "Some in the audience wept openly as Mr Rudd shared painful stories of children he'd spoken with – children who were beaten with belt buckles and bamboo, raped and grew up in places they called 'utterly loveless.'"

The apology from Prime Minister Rudd came two days after British Prime Minister Gordon Brown said he would issue an apology early in 2010 to all child migrants deported from Britain.

6. MOTHERS AND CHILDREN WITHOUT CHOICES

Wartime mothers who could not afford to keep their children without working had little choice but to give up their children. The WWII mothers' decision to evacuate their children made it possible for them to work for the war effort. The British government did not investigate the effects of the evacuation. Similarly, they did not investigate, until forced to the deportation of the thousands of children they "sold" to colonial governments. Many of today's researchers would agree that the children in the British deportation schemes and the children who were evacuated were treated as commodities, separated from their parents without a thought given to their feelings. The British government objective was not always "in the best interest of the children," but rather "in the best interest of the country."

The British government, which sold its children until 1967, does not want to publicly to acknowledge WWII evacuees who also received long-term suffering as a result of abuse from their host families or separation from their parents. The original intent was to take the children from the danger zones and place them in safer areas. The government had no excuse that they were unaware of what the repercussions of such an evacuation would be on these child evacuees.

Steve Davies, a psychologist and lecturer at the University of Hertfordshire, School of Psychology, has examined the long-term psychological effects of the Second World War Home Front and developed an ongoing research programme into the lifespan impact of the U.K. Wartime Child Evacuation programme. I wrote to Davies explaining that I was writing a book about my evacuation experience and was interested in his findings on the effects of the experience on former evacuees. He replied:

> I share your feelings about the deafening silence about evacuees' experiences and questions after the war. The general argument that we didn't know anything about what would happen to children who were evacuated at the time really doesn't hold water. Drs. John Bowlby and Donald Winnicott, both eminent psychotherapists at the Tavistock Clinic in London, wrote to the British Medical Journal and the Times in the summer of 1939 saying that mass evacuation of unaccompanied children was a bad idea for their mental health. It seems that they were ignored.

> Interestingly, a report produced about the Glasgow evacuation programme by Dr. McIntosh, the public health director for the area in 1944 and funded by the Commonwealth Fund warned that the psychological aspects of the evacuation programme had not been done well, and services would need to be available when the evacuees returned at the end of the war. This advice also seems to have been ignored, by the authorities at the time.

> I would like to say that it is all different now but I am still conferring regularly with colleagues in the mental health professions. Evacuation experiences are not asked about or thought relevant when older people come to their doctors or others in distress. We still have a way to go.

Ruth Inglis, an author and former evacuee, explained, "In psychiatric terms, many adult evacuees have 'internalized" their experience; they batten down the hatches of their grief and separation anxiety at the time of being evacuated, but every time they are parted from a child, the experience is relived, making the parting doubly painful."[61]

Ruth Inglis quoted Margaret Hanton, an evacuee who was separated for over five years from her mother. The experience resulted in making her indecisive in later life. Margaret could make the important decisions, "but simple ones wrack her soul. Purchasing any large item throws her into turmoil: when buying a car, deciding on the make hurls her into a confusion which far outweighs whatever is at stake."[62] Ruth Inglis said she could identify with her. I could also.

Alone, I have organized and completed family moves from Germany to England or England to the United States. In 1966 before my husband returned from Vietnam, he asked me to buy a new car. It was a daunting task. One of his fellow USAF pilots who came back early from South East Asia helped me to make the purchase. Similarly, after my husband died I agonized for a year trying to decide on a new car before I finally bought it.

In 2008, I attended a poetry-writing workshop where we were asked to write a poem. I wrote about a rug ruined when a bathroom toilet overflowed. The colors on the rug bled and the restorer said, "We cannot repair it." The last line of my poem read, "I mourned its passing." Each participant commented on every poem. One woman summed up the consensus on mine saying, "There is so much sadness in your poem. It is hard to believe you are writing about a rug."

Throughout my life, any loss was extremely difficult and it was hard to say goodbye. In later years, a summertime visit to Devon to visit my mother was pleasurable, but the leaving was agonizing. When my children went to a new school, I lay awake the night before in a panic about the coming day. I experienced each event with more emotion than it probably warranted. For me this was a normal reaction. As children, we learn to deal with trauma and loss and carry that template into our adult lives.

Dr. John Bowlby and Dr. Donald Winnicott explained to the government what the repercussions would be prior to the start of the evacuation. IN 1944, Dr. MacIntosh told them that, after the war, the returning evacuee children would need special care. The government ignored the warnings that could have helped the children to better adjust to their future lives. The British government's history of child migration was abusive. Not taking care of the needs of children separated from their parents was equally abusive.

In 1987, Dr. John Bowlby repeated his 1939 opinion about the negative affect of the evacuation when he told the London Sunday Times, "The evacuation was a bad mistake and it was the child guidance people who had pick up the pieces. The result was the writing into the education bill of 1944, The Butler Act, that there be, 'a child guidance service throughout the country.'" [63]

7. LESSONS AND LULLABIES

While the WW II evacuation is reputed to be the catalyst for the British social and National Health programs that benefited future generations, to my knowledge, there were no programs developed to support evacuees, traumatized by the evacuation experience. Children, physically, mentally or sexually abused had to find their own way to live with their trauma.

There were few studies conducted on evacuee children after the war. However, in 1950 Richard Titmus launched the academic subject of Social Administration. Although Titmus had great influence on social policy and social work, he had no formal academic training. From a rural farming background, he had left school at the age of 14, the normal leaving age for children of the era, and worked for 16 years in the insurance industry. He wrote on a variety of social issues and his work received national recognition. He was an official war historian and his report, *Problems of Social Policy*, which included an account of the evacuation, gained him a solid reputation and the chair of Social Administration at the London School of Economics from 1950 to his death in 1973. [64]

However, contemporary WWII researchers, including Steve Davies, did not think his report included in-depth data of the kind useful for contemporary researchers—perhaps a result of Titmus' lack of an academic research background.

In 2003, Davies, from the University of Hertfordshire, led the first team that studied former evacuees. He found some disturbing patterns.

It is always difficult to be certain about research data when it is collected retrospectively. When you ask people to cast their minds back there is inevitable "leakage" into their memories from other experiences....Our minds always edit things to some extent. So whilst we cannot be sure about the results of our studies some themes do emerge and they do so in a way that we would expect for children who were separated from their families, often at a young age, and placed with strangers, often for long periods of time. There seem to be some effects on how these evacuees have got on with close partners as adults. University College London, clinical psychology doctoral student, Diane Foster's study found that former evacuees generally felt less happy and satisfied with their romantic relationships as adults than some people, who were not evacuated. They also seem to be in relatively poorer mental health as older people. University College London, clinical psychology doctoral student, Melinda Waugh's study seemed to indicate that evacuees were reporting high rates of experiences that child protection agencies probably would say were abusive or neglectful at the hands of adults during the evacuation. I feel that this was probably due to a lack of psychological mindedness on the part of the main organisers of the formal evacuation scheme.

They were very efficient at preventing loss of life through careful timetabling of "E" [Evacuation] Day and beyond in 1939, but delivered unaccompanied children to entirely unsuitable locations to be billeted with (some) entirely unsuitable adults. I don't think the authorities would contemplate something like this today, not if they wanted to stay in government. Any child protection and welfare agencies would never let it happen in the fashion that it did then. [65]

Davies also spoke about older children given responsibility for younger siblings and told, "Stay with your brothers and sisters and don't let anyone separate you." In many cases, siblings went to different homes and the older child suffered from continuing guilt. They lived with the fact that they had been helpless and had not been responsible.

Such events caused child evacuees to learn helplessness and a feeling of inevitability [a behavior called Learned Helplessness – considered a risk for depression] saying such things as, "Why try when I have no control over what happens to me?" The former evacuees often stigmatized themselves, a trait they may have learned as children. Children of the era knew to keep a 'Stiff Upper Lip' and not talk about their experiences.[66]

According to Dr. Stuart Rusby, Dr. Bowlby's warnings about not sending children away without their mothers before they were five-years-old was prophetic.

> He was concerned about their psychological health. These were prophetic words. From my own research, the effects are seen in a propensity to insecure adult attachment disorders such as depression and clinical anxiety. Not surprisingly, this has also led to high levels of divorce. These negative effects are also associated with the quality of care experienced in foster homes.

> On a more positive note, what is interesting is that overall I found no significant effects between those who were, and those who were not evacuated. What this tells us is that in my sample of some 900 respondents the positive outcome for those older children 'made up' for those of a younger age. It is only when you look in detail at the evacuation experience in terms of age, quality of care, length of time away and frequency of parental visits, that you discern the real picture. Some older children from an urban background certainly benefitted from the broad experience gained, particularly if their parents were able to maintain contact with them. [67]

8. INJURED FATHERS AND INJURED CHILDREN

For me, having a stepfather injured in World War I made for a life significantly influenced by two World Wars. My stepfather was fighting his own demons, with a diagnosis of neurasthenia, (PTSD). No one explained that to me. The government that sent him to fight the war as a teenager did not help him to adjust to life with the injuries he sustained. Unfortunately, he did not receive any help for the physical or mental injuries he received from his WWI service. Nor did I have help or anyone to explain my evacuation experience. The fact that my stepfather didn't speak when I came home from school in the evenings made for unhappy teenage years. He knew nothing about relating to children and he wanted my mother's attention when she was home.

My brother never came to live with us, so I was in fact an only child. From a young age, I was a depressed child incapable of living life in the moment and enjoying life as it was happening. I usually found myself on the outside of groups. It was like standing outside a house and looking through the window into the lives of others. In order not be sent away again, I learned early to put on a smile to cover all situations - happy or sad.

Being away from home at such a young age, I was excessively independent. Throughout my life, I never asked anyone to do what I was capable of doing myself. I cannot remember not bathing or dressing myself or plaiting my own hair. I worked hard to excel in everything: ballet, education, behavior or appearance. A friend's mother told me at a party I was the perfect guest because I was a good loser – "she loses with a smile." I tried to be "perfect" in all ways. They didn't send "perfect" children away.

I did well in my schoolwork and passed the scholarship exam the first time I took it. Clifton College offered me a place. I thought it would be a wonderful experience for me because it would have taken me away from my stepfather and his silence. Mother did not want me to go away to school again. Unfortunately, through no fault of her own, she was never able to be there in the evenings for me. She worked very hard as a night nurse to support the family. She left for work when I arrived home from school and came home the next morning when

I was leaving for school. She also worked most weekends. I knew she worked hard and felt an obligation not to leave home.

Mother never told me she loved me nor did she hug me –her family simply did not do that – but I always knew she did. She showed it in many ways, such as buying items for me when she had little money and ignoring her own needs. My parents did not attend school events, but occasionally, when she could, mother came to see me dance.

As an adult, major decisions were not hard for me to make, but relatively minor things – buying that car, for example – weighed heavily, as though one little slip could have implications I was unable to see. Saying goodbye for any reason was something I would rather not face – it was, and is, always hard. Death and loss of any kind is difficult for me to accept.

While I did well nursing my husband for the almost two years of his illness, his death was something I was able to deny for an extended period of time. He had brought me to a foreign land and promised he would always take care of me. Wayne and I had talked every day for our entire forty-year marriage, wherever he was in the world, with the exception of his two-year tours in Vietnam. We talked only once in 1966, a rather unsatisfying conversation via Ham Radio. In later years, I also talked daily with my husband's father, Glenn Lehr.

My husband, age 64, died on 16 July 2001, and his father, age 93, died on 20 July 2001. I lost my two closest confidants in one week. I do not think anyone realized how completely devastated I was by those two losses. The smile to cover every contingency served me well.

A man with whom I recently discussed the subject of my book said he was "surprised I wasn't a 'basket case.'" Another said, "I want to shake your hand because I am amazed that you can recount such painful issues in such a calm and collected manner."

I had a lot of practice – from the age of three years I watched and assessed the moods of the people around me. I learned to recognize their needs above my own. It was a matter of survival.

9. 'CHILDHOODS DO MATTER'

On 15 October 2008, Dr. Jay Belsky, director of the Institute for the Study of Children, Families and Social issues and Professor of Psychology at the University of London, gave an interview to BBC Radio One's "Family Affair" programme entitled "Legacy of Childhood on Attachment Security in Aging Adults." Belsky discussed his belief "that what happens early in life matters to how children turn out, not just in early childhood, or middle childhood, or even adolescence but well beyond."

He cited the challenge to scientists to be around long enough to gather data on individuals from childhood to maturity. Belsky addressed the research by Stuart Rusby and Fiona Tasker on 1,467 individuals between the ages of 62 to 72, evacuated as children from their homes in Kent. These former WWII evacuees went to host families in South Wales, Devon and Cornwall.[68]

Stuart and Tasker compared evacuated children to similar numbers of individuals who were not evacuated, and concluded it was men who were more likely to consider not being too close to others as important, and not being inclined to share their feelings. The age of the children at the time of evacuation was also a factor. Children evacuated between the ages of four and six increased the likelihood of men and women not being secure in late adulthood.

Davies and Rusby agreed with Belsky that what happened to evacuated children did affect them throughout their lives. For some individuals the problems did not reveal themselves until the former evacuees were of retirement age. With more time to think through issues they had been able to "push down" in their busier earlier lives were now beginning to surface. Parsons has said that the result of testing on evacuated German and Finnish children has revealed similar findings.

> Rusby wrote that, "In a sense it is a reminder that in the first years of life the security engendered by parental love is crucial to secure development and eventual maturity. The WWII British government was concerned by the need for physical security [of the evacuee children] to the loss of emotional security. It does also underline the need for professionalism in monitoring foster placements, and the importance of parental contact when children are taken into care. It reminds mental health professionals too of their need to consider the quality of their childhood upbringing when treating adults."

Establishing a link between the separation of young children from their primary caregivers and lifetime problems has value for future children and child development professionals. Even given the fact that, as Stephen Davies stated, "It is always difficult to be certain about research when it is collected retrospectively," the data from so many individuals is important. It is necessary to gather such data before former evacuees are no longer around.

In October 2009, The Center for Disease Control's (CDC) David W. Brown DSc, MScPH, and colleagues reported that people who experienced multiple childhood traumas may be at increased risk of early death. They reported that "those who had six or more traumatic events as children – including emotional, physical, or sexual abuse – died almost 20 years earlier than patients who hadn't suffered childhood trauma."[69] This CDC report is further validation that childhoods do matter.

Evacuee research provides a valuable tool for health professionals and childcare departments to ensure that young children keep contact with their parents, or a substitute caregiver, in the first years of their lives. Children moved from one foster family to another, may have similar security issues throughout their lives.

When I asked Stuart Rusby to recommend others conducting research in the field of evacuee children he said, "There is very little work in this field. Steve [Davies] has no doubt given you references to two papers written by two of his students [Diane Foster and Melinda Waugh]," but that was the extent of his suggestions. Martin Parsons also commented on the dearth of individuals working in the field. In September 2006 he conducted a conference at Reading University on Children and War where there were participants from a variety of countries.

It was encouraging also to note that on 5 April 2009, Rutgers University held a conference with the same title, now in its second year. Conference director Lynne Vallone, chair of the Department of Childhood Studies, said, "The roles children play, and have played, during wartime is a topic that cries out for historicizing and in-depth investigation."

At the 2009 Rutger's conference, Ishmael Beah, author of the memoir, *A Long Way Gone*, which chronicles his time on the Sierra Leone battlefield at the age of 13, delivered the keynote address. Michael Wessells, a professor of psychology at Columbia University and Randolf-Macon College, author of *Child Soldiers: From Violence to Protection*, discussed his findings on girl soldiers. These speakers give a powerful message about how even today children are abused by governments—in this case, by using them as combatants. It is encouraging to note that conference presenters were from Yale University, Oxford University and the University of Calgary, a signal that academic inquiry in this field is beginning to grow in importance.

As Vallone said, "the conference is the first of many more high-impact events designed to expand the student experience and broaden the global conversation on children. Childhood studies offer the promise of a much richer discussion and understanding on a range of issues impacting children – war is just a start."

Dr. Martin Parsons has repeatedly said, "War children are invisible."

We could add that many groups of children have been invisible throughout the generations. With the many wars taking place throughout the world, increased numbers of children's lives are negatively impacted. The encouragement of researchers to study all children affected by war will help to alleviate the problems of past generations.

Only when researchers examine the lives of children, particularly in exploitive situations such as abuse, evacuation, migrations and war, will those children become visible. It is important to rediscovered, reassembled and examine those childhoods—much as I have done in this book with mine.

FOOTNOTES

[1] Davies, Jennifer, *The Wartime Kitchen and Garden*, BBC Books, London, 1993, 99.

[2] Jackson, Carlton, *Who Will Take Our Children*, Methuen, London, 1985, 39.

[3] Davies, 19-20

[4] Ibid, 20.

[5] Ibid, 20

[6] Along with the official documents about the evacuation several authors have written accounts about E (Evacuation) Day: Parsons, Martin L, *I'll Take That One, Dispelling the Myths of Civilian Evacuation*, Becket & Karlson, Peterborough, 1998. Wicks, Ben, *No Time To Wave Goodbye*, Bloomsbury, London, 1988. Inglis Ruth, *The Children's War*, Collins, London, 1989.

[7] Conversation in Cambridge, England with Ret. Air Commodore, Derek Hine, 1988.

[8] Conversation with Doreen (Gallagher) Stafford, Devon, England 1997.

[9] MacMillan, Margaret, *Women of the Raj*, Random House, New York, 1998, 159-160

[10] Stokes, Edward, *Innocents Abroad, the story of British child evacuees in Australis*, 1940-45, Allen & Unwin, London, 1994, 49.

[11] Accounts of the sinking of the Andora Star, Volendam and The City of Benares, are recorded by Inglis,1989; Parsons, 1998; Stokes, 1994; and Wicks, 1988.

[12] Wicks, 1989, 3.

[13] Parsons, 171.

[14] It had been difficult for me to establish the date that I went to the Methodist Boy's School. The only marker we have is that Uncle Howard came to visit me before he left for Egypt – according to my Aunt Hazel he returned when the war with Europe was over in 1945. She said he had been away for five years. If he left in 1940, I would have been three years old. I left the school after my father's death in December 1942.

[15] Clay, F.F. with colleagues and students, *The Grovian: 175th Anniversary Supplement 1812-1987*, Woodhouse Grove School, Apperley Bridge, Yorkshire, 1987, 3.

[16] Clay, 3.

[17] Freud and Burlingham, *War and Children*, Medical War Books, London, 1943, 119-120.

[18] Ian Goldthorpe, *Grassington and the surrounding villages Toward the Millenium*, The Dales Book Centre, North Yorkshire, England, 1998, 30.

[19] Davies, Jennifer, *The Wartime Kitchen and Garden; The Home Front 1939-45*, BBC Books, London, 1995, 56.

[20] Ibid, 25

[21] Ibid, 55

22 Ibid, 142

[23] Ella Pontefract & Mary Hartley, *Wharfedale*, Smith Settle, Otley, 1938, 153.

[24] Ibid, 48

[25] 27 March 2009 conversation with James Roffey.

[26] August 1998 *The Evacuee*.

[27] In fact, in the February 2009 edition of *The Evacuee*, James Roffey expressed his gratitude to Leopard Films for making *The Evacuees Reunited*, a series broadcast on ITV. The filmmakers worked in conjunction with James and were true to their word when they promised to show an accurate depiction of the evacuation. Leopard Films, *The Evacuees Reunion*, ITV Television, December 15-19 2008.

[28] The information on the evacuation was reported in government documents and has been repeated by various sources including Wikipedia, Internet essays by researchers and schoolchildren study WWII evacuation, as well as by Martin L. Parsons, Ruth Inglis and Stuart Rusby.

[29] Parsons, Martin L., *I'll Take That One: Dispelling the Myths of Civilian Evacuation 1939-45*, Peterborough, Cambs, 1998, 17.

[30] Parsons, 113.

[31] Boorman, John, *Hope and Glory*, Boorman, director and evacuee, 1987. The New York Times said it was hard to imagine war as "idyllic" – but not impossible after viewing Boorman's film.

[32] Schweitzer Pam, Andy Andrews, Pat Fawcett, eds., *Goodnight Children Everywhere: Memories of Evacuation in World War II*, Age Exchange Theatre Trust, 1990, 31.

[33] Kops, Bernard, *The World is a Wedding*, Inpress Books, London, 2007, 31-32.

[34] *Goodnight Children Everywhere*, 36-37.

[35] 27 March 2009 conversation with James Roffey.

[36] Parsons, 18.

[37] Martin Parsons, lecture, Evacuees, Internet Self-Access Centre for Language Learning SACLL, 31 May 2006. Recordings on a variety of topics by university lecturers for access by students, researchers.

[38] Pinchbeck, Ivy, & Margaret Hewitt, *Children in English Society: From the Nineteenth Century to the Children's Act*, Routledge & Kegan Paul, London.

[39] Office of Public Sector Information, Children and Young Persons Act, 1933 (c.12). London, 2003-2004.

[40] Ivy Pinchbeck & Margaret Hewett, Children in English Society: From the Nineteenth Century to the Children's Act.

[41] Kingsley, Charles, *Water Babies: A Fairy Tale for a Land Baby*, written originally as a serial for MacMillan's Magazine, London, 1863 and later published as a book that remained popular for children well into the 20th century. Kinsley wrote the story for his son.

[42] Blake, William, *Song of Innocence: The Chimney Sweeper*, London, 1789. (Blake was author and printer).

[43] International Association of Former Child Migrants and Their Families Senate Community Affairs References Committee Submission, Australia, 2001, 13.

[44] Ibid, 17.

[45] Snow, Perry, *Neither Waif Nor Stray: The Search for a Stolen Identity*, Universal Publishers, 2000.

[46] Ibid

[47] Public Broadcasting Service, *The American Experience: The Orphan Trains*, (transcript), David McCullough, Host. 1995, 1.

[48] Ibid, 2-3.

[49] Ibid, 3.

[50] Ibid,4.

[51] Ibid,5.

[52] Boyles, Denis, Superior Nebraska, Doubleday, 2008.

[53] Bean, Philip, and Joy Melville, *Lost Children of the Empire*, Unwin Hayes, London, 1989. The book was dramatized in a television documentary. In 1992, the Australian Broadcasting Company (ABC) and the British Broadcasting Company (BBC) co-sponsored a television mini-series also based on the book, *The Leaving of Liverpool*.

[54] The United Kingdom Parliament, House of Commons – Select Committee on Health – Third Report, 3/15/2009, 1.

[55] Australian Broadcasting Company (ABC) Television, Lateline Stories, Sins Of The Brothers, Maxine McKew opened the program with the remark: "For thousands of British children it was the ultimate betrayal." David Ransom narrated the Scottish documentary as part of the programme. He related the following on page 4 of the transcript, ..the sorry saga of British Child Migration – child labor – paedophilia, which the recent House of Commons report describes as: .."quite exceptional depravity so that terms like 'sexual abuse' are too weak to convey it," 4.

[56] Humphreys, Margaret, *Empty Cradles*, Doubleday, London, 1994. Ms. Humphreys is credited with single handedly bring the Child Migration issue to the attention of the British and Australian governments as well as the general public in both countries. Her book was a contributing factor in educating people on the issue.

[57] Ibid, 2.

[58] Ibid, 4.

[59] The International Association of Former Child Migrants and Their Families, Section 2, Child Migrants – Who Are We? Myth Number 3 – Children deported to Australia were war orphans or unwanted street urchins, 15.

[60] Ibid, 15.

[61] Inglis, Ruth, *The Children's War: Evacuation 1939-1945*, Collins, London, 162.

[62] Ibid, 162.

[63] John Bowlby (1907-1990) his Attachment Theory, is credited with being one of the most influential theories of the Twentieth century. Bowlby opined that a child's early tie to the mother and its disruption through separation, deprivation, and bereavement affects them over their lifetime. Bowlby warned the British government prior to 1939 that the evacuation would create long term problems for the child evacuees.

[64] Oakley, Ann, *Man & Wife: Richard & Kay Titmuss: My Parent's Early Years*, Harper Collins, London, 1996.

[65] Correspondence from Steve Davies 27 March 2009.

[66] Ibid.

[67] Correspondence from Dr. Rusby April 06, 2009.

[68] Rusby, J.S.M., *Childhood Temporary Separation: Long-term Effects of Wartime Evacuation in World War 2*, Dissertation. com, Boca Raton, Florida, USA, 2005.

[69] Kristina Fiore, "Trauma During Childhood Could Shorten Lifespan," Medpage Today, reviewed by Robert Jasmer, MD Associate Clinical Professor of Medicine, University of California, San Francisco, October 2009.

QUESTIONS FOR DISCUSSION

1. What was the code name of the British World War II evacuation of approximately three million women and children? Britain was not invaded, so why did the government consider it important to evacuate people from major cities and towns?

2. How many official government evacuations were there? How successful was the first evacuation? What did the British people call the early days of the war, and why?

3. What were the ages of evacuee children, and what were they required to carry with them at all times? How were the children identified?

4. Could parents travel with their evacuated children and did they know their offsprings' destinations? How did many parents respond to their children being taken away? Why did parents respond more readily to later evacuations?

5. The government subcommittee on evacuation consisted of men led by Lord Portal. How different might the evacuation have been if women had been included in the decision making process?

6. Did Prime Minister Winston Churchill approve of overseas evacuations? Were Princesses Elizabeth and Margaret Rose, the daughters of King George and Queen Elizabeth, evacuated?

7. How many children drowned on the ship *The City of Benares*? What affect did those deaths have on the official government overseas evacuations? How did the general public react to the £25 cost per child for the overseas evacuation?

8. How did the USA come to the aid of the British in 1941? What precipitated this action? What was it called and how important was it?

9. How many schools were built specifically for evacuee children and what was their alternate purpose if the war did not occur?

10. Did you know about the migration of British children until 1967 or the Orphan Trains in America prior to reading this book? If not, discuss your opinions about the fact that governments took this action usually without the parents' permission.

11. Did you have a preconceived opinion of the economic and social status of British evacuees? Why do you think the British government thought that separating women from their children would be acceptable to the average parent?

12. With the information now available do you think the evacuation was a success? Looking through the lens of wartime Britain, the bombings, the threat of German

invasion, how do you think you would have responded to your children being removed from your care?

13. The British government made extensive preparation for the evacuation but despite professional advice that the children would be negatively affected by the experience little valid data was collected and no assistance was given to the children. How do you think the lives of these children could have been improved if they had received post-evacuation help?

ABOUT THE AUTHOR

◇◇◇

Doreen Drewry Lehr, Ph.D., a British World War II evacuee has published articles but this is her first book. She married Wayne R. Lehr, a US Air Force Officer in 1961. She has lived in England, Germany, many of the US States and has traveled extensively. Ms. Lehr taught at Springfield College, Manchester, New Hampshire, and Western Michigan University, Kalamazoo, Michigan. A Gold Star Wife, with two children and two grandchildren, she lives in Washington, DC and Key West, Florida.

Photo Courtesy of Richard Watherwax

INDEX

◇◇◇◇◇◇◇◇◇◇◇◇◇◇◇◇◇◇◇◇◇

TreeNeutral™

Lightning Source UK Ltd.
Milton Keynes UK
01 September 2010

159301UK00007B/77/P